P9-BJC-200

Praise for

SLAVERY, CIVIL WAR, AND SALVATION

"*Slavery, Civil War, and Salvation* is an important challenge to the claim that Christianity was the central faith and culture of African American slaves. Taking the words of African Americans from both before and after the Civil War seriously, Daniel L. Fountain suggests that most slaves did not convert to Christianity. Instead, religious diversity and variety characterized their lives in the antebellum South. The move to Christianity occurred after the war. If Fountain is right, then scholars of American religion and African American history have much new terrain to survey. The complexities of life in slavery and freedom continue to reveal so much to those with curious eyes and sensitive souls."

—EDWARD J. BLUM, author of *Reforging the White Republic: Race, Religion, and American Nationalism, 1865–1898*

"Daniel L. Fountain challenges the conventional wisdom that Christianity played a central role in the slave community, although a 'Christian core' among the enslaved prophesied that God would deliver them out of slavery. Only after the Civil War brought that promised emancipation, he concludes, did African Americans become Christians in large numbers. With its provocative new interpretation, *Slavery, Civil War, and Salvation* is a 'must read' for everyone interested in the history of African American Christianity or American slavery."

—GAINES M. FOSTER, author of *Moral Reconstruction: Christian Lobbyists and the Federal Legislation of Morality, 1865–1920*

During the Civil War, traditional history tells us, Afro-Christianity proved a strong force for slaves' perseverance and hope of deliverance. In *Slavery, Civil War, and Salvation*, however, Daniel Fountain raises the possibility that Afro-Christianity played a less significant role within the antebellum slave community than most scholars currently assert. Bolstering his argument with a quantitative survey of religious behavior and WPA slave narratives, Fountain presents a new timeline for the African American conversion experience.

Both the survey and the narratives reveal that fewer than 40 percent of individuals who gave a datable conversion experience had become Christians prior to acquiring freedom. Fountain pairs the survey results with an in-depth examination of the obstacles within the slaves' religious landscape that made conversion more difficult if not altogether unlikely, including infrequent access to religious instruction, the inconsistent Christian message offered to slaves, and the slaves' evolving religious identity. Furthermore, he provides other possible explanations for beliefs that on the surface resembled Christianity but in fact adhered to traditional African religions.

Fountain maintains that only after emancipation and the fulfillment of the predicted Christian deliverance did African Americans more consistently turn to Christianity. Freedom, Fountain contends, brought most former slaves into the Christian faith. Provocative and enlightening, *Slavery, Civil War, and Salvation* redefines the role of Christianity within the slave community.

Kevin Niles

DANIEL L. FOUNTAIN
is an associate professor of history and director of the public history program at Meredith College in Raleigh, North Carolina.

Slavery, Civil War, and Salvation

CONFLICTING WORLDS

New Dimensions of the American Civil War

T. Michael Parrish, Series Editor

SLAVERY
CIVIL WAR

AND

SALVATION

AFRICAN AMERICAN SLAVES AND
CHRISTIANITY, 1830–1870

DANIEL L. FOUNTAIN

LOUISIANA STATE UNIVERSITY PRESS

BATON ROUGE

Published by Louisiana State University Press
Copyright © 2010 by Louisiana State University Press
All rights reserved
Manufactured in the United States of America
First printing

DESIGNER: Michelle A. Neustrom
TYPEFACES: Rosewood, display; Chaparral Pro, text
PRINTER: McNaughton & Gunn, Inc.
BINDER: John H. Dekker & Sons

Earlier versions of chapters 2 and 4 were published as "Christ in Chains: Slavery's Negative Impact on the Conversion of African American Slaves," in *Affect & Power: Essays on Sex,
Slavery, Race, and Religion in Appreciation of Winthrop Jordan*, ed. David J. Libby, Paul Spick-
ard, and Susan Ditto (Jackson: University Press of Mississippi, 2005), 84–104, and "Christ
Unchained: African American Conversions during the Civil War Era," *Ohio Valley History* 3
(Summer 2003): 31–46, respectively, and are reprinted by permission of the editors. Some
material in chapter 3 appeared earlier in the *Journal of Interdisciplinary History* 26 (1995):
66–77. It is included herein with the permission of the editors of The Journal of Interdisciplinary History and The MIT Press, Cambridge, Massachusetts. Copyright © 1995 by the
Massachusetts Institute of Technology and The Journal of Interdisciplinary History, Inc.

LIBRARY OF CONGRESS CATALOGING-IN-PUBLICATION DATA

Fountain, Daniel L., 1967–
    Slavery, Civil War, and salvation : African American slaves and
Christianity, 1830–1870 / Daniel L. Fountain.
        p. cm. — (Conflicting worlds)
    Includes bibliographical references and index.
    ISBN 978-0-8071-3699-7 (cloth : alk. paper) 1. Slaves—Religious
life—Southern States—History—19th century. 2. African Amer-
icans—Southern States—Religion—History—19th century. 3.
Slavery and the church—Southern States—History—19th century.
4. Christian converts—Southern States—History. 5. Southern
States—Religious life and customs. 6. Slave narratives—Southern
States—History and criticism. I. Title.
    E443.F68 2010
    261.8—dc22
                                                    2010006967

The paper in this book meets the guidelines for permanence and durability
of the Committee on Production Guidelines for Book Longevity
of the Council on Library Resources. ∞

To Winthrop D. Jordan:
you are missed.

CONTENTS

PREFACE

I first began to consider the role that alternative faiths might have played in the antebellum slave community during a graduate seminar on southern religion taught by Charles Reagan Wilson at the University of Mississippi. Further fueled by readings on comparative religion that I encountered in Douglas Sullivan-Gonzalez's seminar on Latin American history, I decided to approach Winthrop D. Jordan with the idea of surveying slave narratives to determine the degree of African American conversion to Christianity. I drew up a proposal based on my work in those two classes and set up a meeting with Win to discuss the viability of this survey as part of a study of slave religion. Win was skeptical but listened intently as I explained what I wanted to do. In the end he signed off on the project but intimated that I was likely to find what others had already gone to great lengths to describe. Still, we both believed that even if my work confirmed earlier findings for the dominance of Afro-Christianity, the survey would allow me to give a more detailed description of the slave Christian community and perhaps reveal regional differences where they occurred. With Win's caveats in mind, I began scouring the thousands of surviving slave narratives to see what would emerge.

I distinctly remember the excitement I felt as the findings presented here started to take shape. When I completed the survey, I raced to tell Win that my survey revealed that more than 60 percent of the slaves surveyed indicated that they were not Christians while enslaved. His response floored me. Win rose from his chair, smiled at me, and said, "Dan, that's nifty!" I must admit I expected something different from the man who wrote *White over Black: American Attitudes Toward the Negro, 1550–1812*, but that moment has become priceless to me as a reminder of his warmth and unpredictability. What followed was predictable, however, as Win quizzed me on the sources I would tackle next and made several recommendations on must-reads. That was ten years ago, and his insistence that I go to the sources and keep digging has driven my work ever since.

I cannot honestly say that Win was fully convinced by my findings, nifty or not, but he did come to believe that it was a real possibility that most antebellum slaves were not Christians. He admitted that his own work on Adams County, Mississippi, in *Tumult and Silence at Second Creek: An Inquiry into a Civil War Slave Conspiracy* had revealed very little evidence of Christianity within the conspirator community he studied. I remain thankful for and gratified by his admission as well as his openness to testing established interpretation. As it did with Win, I know that the speculative argument presented here will face skepticism in the wake of several decades' worth of research written by thoughtful, serious scholars who see a different religious landscape among the antebellum slave community. We have learned much from them about the meaning of Afro-Christianity, and I, and many other scholars, remain in their debt. I hope that readers will see my work not as a refutation of earlier works but as an attempt to open new avenues of inquiry about Afro-Christianity and bring greater focus on the members of the slave community who did not embrace that faith. While my work suggests that fewer slaves converted to Christianity, it also identifies the faith as the dynamic force that came to dominate the African American community after emancipation. As such, I see the interpretation here as an affirmation of the Christian slaves' creativity and dedication that so many have identified and celebrated. In other words, while my work attempts to offer an alternative explanation about when, why, and to what degree most slaves converted to Christianity, there is also plenty about previous interpretations that I find commendable and embrace.

There are many people who helped bring this project to fruition and to whom I owe many thanks. To begin, I would like to thank the University Press of Mississippi and the Filson Historical Society as earlier versions of chapters 2 and 4 previously appeared in *Affect & Power: Essays on Sex, Slavery, Race, and Religion in Appreciation of Winthrop Jordan* (2005) and in the Summer 2003 issue of *Ohio Valley History,* respectively. A portion of chapter 3 was published in an article I wrote for the *Journal of Interdisciplinary History* in 1995 and appears here courtesy of the same. The University of Mississippi, the University of Mississippi History Department, and the Southern Baptist Historical Library and Archives each provided funding that allowed me to travel and conduct research. Winthrop D. Jordan, Ted Ownby, Charles Reagan Wilson, and Robbie F. Ethridge provided me great latitude and excellent guidance throughout the research and writing process. In addition, the book has benefited from several good friends who took time away from their own work to read and offer advice on some of the chapters. Steve Budney, Jay Gillispie, Mike Butler, and Kathi McMahon, I truly appreciate your generosity. I am also grateful to my former colleagues Jennifer Mangum and Rodney Allen, at the Louisiana School for Math, Science, and the Arts, who reviewed my quantitative methodology and findings as well as gave me editorial advice. Edward J. Blum and Gaines M. Foster provided thoughtful feedback on earlier drafts of chapters as members of a panel during a conference sponsored by the Society for the Scientific Study of Religion. The History and Political Science Department and the Dean of Humanities and Social Sciences at Meredith College provided guidance and emotional support as I pursued publication of this manuscript. I am particularly grateful for the assistance William S. Price gave me in finding outside readers who were incredibly generous and helpful. Of those, Donald G. Mathews and Laurie Maffly-Kipp of the University of North Carolina at Chapel Hill deserve special thanks.

Finally, I want to thank my family for their support. The Fountains and Fanas have been phenomenally supportive and patient with me as this project took shape. In particular, I want to thank my lovely wife Michele and son Tait, who have put up with me through many days of research, writing, and editing. Without you, this book would have never come to pass, and I appreciate your patience and enthusiasm for my work. I love you both more than you will ever know.

Slavery, Civil War, and Salvation

INTRODUCTION

William E. Montgomery's fine study of the African American church in the postbellum South informs readers that nineteenth-century whites often condescendingly described black worship as "long on religion and short on Christianity."[1] Such a statement reflects the general contempt that most white Christians held for the animated worship services of many African American churches. In contrast to this negative view, I embrace this phrase as a means of encouraging others to consider alternative interpretations about the degree of Christianity that existed within the antebellum slave community. More precisely, my research into slave religious practices has forced me to consider the possibility that while most nineteenth-century African American slaves had some form of religious belief, they were not Christians. Emancipation provided African Americans far more incentive and opportunities to convert to Christianity than ever existed under slavery. In outlining the evidence to support such an argument, I join a growing list of scholars such as Allan D. Austin, Sylviane A. Diouf, Michael A. Gomez, Yvonne P. Chireau, Joseph M. Murphy, and Anthony B. Pinn, all of whom emphasize the existence of religious diversity among the past and present African American population of the United States.[2] This emerging trend flows against the tremendous current of African American religious historiography that concentrates heavily on the role of Christianity within the black community. Not surprisingly, then, the speculative argument presented here raises questions about some of the most widely accepted interpretations about the role of religion within the slave community.

A strong body of literature describes how during slavery, elements of African Traditional Religion merged with Christianity to create a uniquely African American form of the Christian faith. The works of

1

Albert J. Raboteau, Mechal Sobel, and Margaret Washington Creel represent some of the most detailed research that describes the emergence and growth of Afro-Christianity.[3] Their scholarship shows that West African religions contain many beliefs similar to those characterizing the evangelical Christianity that dominated the antebellum southern United States. Among them, both African Traditional Religion and evangelical Christianity emphasize a single creator God, symbolic death and rebirth, water as a spiritual symbol, blood sacrifice, religious prayer and song, and belief in an afterlife.[4]

According to most interpretations of nineteenth-century slave religion, these similarities facilitated the conversion of slaves to Christianity by allowing them to incorporate familiar beliefs into their New World environment. This confluence resulted in a slave-created form of Christianity that reflected African as well as European Christian ideals. Mechal Sobel's study of Afro-Baptists provides excellent descriptions of how and why this religious blending or syncretism took place within the southern slave community. For example, Sobel convincingly argues that the Baptist practice of baptismal immersion made that denomination more attractive for African Americans whose ancestors viewed water as a part of the spirit world.[5] Thus, slaves baptized into the region's Baptist churches probably viewed the ritual not only as an expression of their Christian faith but as an opportunity to commune physically with their heavenly creator. In doing so, African Americans understood and experienced Christianity quite differently from their white brethren and subsequently constituted a consciously unique religious community.

Most slavery scholars, such as Eugene D. Genovese, John W. Blassingame, Lawrence W. Levine, and John B. Boles, argue that Afro-Christianity was the cultural center of the antebellum slave community.[6] While their emphases vary, each of these historians asserts that by the late antebellum period Christianity served as a culturally unifying force within the African American slave community. For example, when speaking of Afro-Christianity, Blassingame notes that their "distinctive culture helped the slaves to develop a strong sense of group solidarity. They united to protect themselves from the most oppressive features of slavery and to preserve their self-esteem."[7] Likewise, Genovese argues that Christian prayer meetings "gave the slaves strength derived from direct communion with God and each other. . . . But above all, the meetings provided a sense of autonomy—of constituting not merely a community unto themselves but a community with leaders of their own choice."[8] According to such interpretations, Afro-Christianity was of primary importance for the organization of daily life and the shaping of antebellum African American identity. These interpretations also imply that a majority of the slave community adhered to the principles of the Afro-Christian faith.

I do not question the development of an Afro-Christian religious synthesis in the antebellum South. In fact, the ideas I would like people to consider and investigate further depend on the existence of a vibrant, dedicated Afro-Christian community. However, my research has raised questions about the idea that after 1830 Afro-Christianity was the cultural centerpiece of the southern slave community. A quantitative survey presented in chapter 1 found that only 38 percent of slaves who left behind some form of narrative indicated that they converted to Christianity prior to emancipation. Chapter 2 supports the survey figure by detailing the numerous barriers to converting slaves to Christianity. The evidence provided in these two chapters, it is hoped, will prompt historians to question or at least reexamine the likelihood that most bondsmen would have heard and accepted the Christian message presented to them.

If, as my survey and the evidence on conversion barriers suggest, most slaves in the late antebellum period were not Christians, questions naturally arise about the interpretation of Afro-Christianity as the culturally unifying focal point of the slave community. I suggest that a religiously diverse antebellum slave community is a plausible alternative to the idea of Afro-Christianity as the centerpiece of antebellum slave life. One possible explanation for how several alternative belief systems could have coexisted alongside Afro-Christianity appears in the third chapter. Finally, I describe how Afro-Christianity came to dominate the African American religious landscape after emancipation delivered the freedom that Christian slaves predicted would come. Viewed in this light, instead of being the slaves' cultural focal point, Afro-Christianity was a dynamic, significant, but nonmajority segment of a religiously pluralistic African American slave community. The book in its entirety presents more detailed evidence hypothesizing about the size, location, and membership of a slave "Christian core."

In making the speculative interpretation outlined above, I am attempting to encourage historians and religion scholars to revisit the way African American religious history has typically been conceptualized. First of all, I hope that my work encourages historians not to read history backward. We must not allow the present status of Christianity within the African American population to influence our interpretations of slave religion in the antebellum South. It is possible that in the wake of the civil rights movement it has been hard for scholars to imagine the African American church as other than at the center of the community. Given the church's role in African American life in the twentieth century and today, it is understandable that this view could influence the way that scholars have written about it. This is especially true since many of the sources scholars rely on for understanding African American spirituality were created in the twentieth century when the church clearly dominated the black religious landscape and was a focal point of community identity. It is unlikely that many twentieth-century African Americans would have emphasized the non-Christian roots of the community, and scholars' enthusiasm for the black church's accomplishments may have led them to follow suit. Nonetheless, we must always be careful to set things in their historical context, which is what I have attempted to do in this book.

Second, I would join others in arguing that the middle passage and slavery did not leave Africans as a religious tabula rasa. I believe that the oral cultures of many African societies allowed their religious traditions to survive, though in a modified form. Africans could and did pass on their beliefs to their children, however imperfect that transmission may have been. The first generations of African Americans lived in a world characterized by a variety of African, Native American, and European influences. These influences, in combination with the conditions under which they lived (plantation, Upper or Lower South, city, etc.), led to cultural sharing that was very likely region- or even community-specific. More precisely, the differing demographic conditions and labor systems of the South yielded regional or local religious patterns that, for the slaves, greatly reflected the cultures of the Africans brought to that part of the United States. It is not impossible to imagine that out of this cultural exchange came new, largely African-based religions that most whites generically labeled as hoodoo and conjure. These new faiths would have represented a consensus of religious ideas and practices that an area's slave population extracted from their parents' and neighbors' belief systems. In the argument that follows, these mixed faiths would have been the strongest tradition within a religiously pluralistic African American culture until the coming of the Civil War.

The above interpretation suggests that Afro-Christianity may have played a different role within the slave community than has been previously assumed. Despite the fact that the faith attracted a significant number of converts during the First and Second Great Awakenings, it is possible that Christianity never replaced African-based religions until the Christian god delivered the freedom his followers had prophesied. In this way, emancipation, rather than the middle passage, served as the death knell for long-held African religious beliefs. The argument I present here is that, under slavery, Christianity probably did not meet most slaves' needs; thus most did not convert. As described in chapter 4, those who did accept Christianity likely did so because of the Christian core's demonstrated faith in the coming of freedom and salvation. This interpretation contrasts with the view of scholars who emphasize the importance of the Africanization of Christianity as being central to attracting slave converts to the faith.[9] Rather, this study suggests that the expectation and delivery of freedom was the leading factor for African American conversion to Christianity. Without the hope of freedom, the ring shouts and baptisms of the Christian core, no matter how African in spirit, were meaningless for most slaves. Thus, while the form of the slaves' Christian worship reflected a preferred African symbolic aesthetic, it was the message and reality of deliverance that brought and kept them together.

∽∾ 1 ∽∾
AFRO-CHRISTIANITY BY THE NUMBERS

The Negroes sobbed and shouted and swayed backward and forward, some with aprons to their eyes, most of them clapping their hands and responding in shrill tones: "Yes God!" "Jesus!" "Savior!" "Bless de Lord, amen," etc.
— MARY BOYKIN CHESNUT, *A Diary from Dixie*

At times I would go to hear preaching among the slaves, not to be converted however, but mainly to hear the moaning and hear the preacher quote the Scriptures. Often, while at work, I tried to go through the motions and intonations of the preacher. I was pretty good at heart but considered a devil by those around me.
— UNIDENTIFIED FREEDMAN in Rawick, *American Slave*

Mary Chesnut's description of a nineteenth-century African American worship service is a familiar image for students of antebellum slave religion. Indeed, the works of scholars such as Albert J. Raboteau and Mechal Sobel effectively use such images to paint vivid portraits of what transpired during Christian slaves' public and private worship. However, despite the considerable progress that historians have made in describing how Christian slaves worshiped, there is a tendency to apply evidence pertaining to a few slave Christians to the general population of slaves. For instance, both Sobel's *Trabelin' On: The Slave Journey to an Afro-Baptist Faith* and Raboteau's *Slave Religion: The "Invisible Institution" in the Antebellum South* treat Christianity as the single most important belief system of mid-nineteenth-century African American slaves. Yet Sobel's own study identifies only 14.3 percent (634,000 of 4,441,830) of antebellum African Americans, north and south, as members of Baptist and Methodist churches. These two religious groups easily claimed the lion's share of the United States' black communicants. Certainly nineteenth-century standards for church membership, which were more stringent than those of later periods, limited the number of slave Christians who were actual church members. Nevertheless, the fact that so very few were members suggests that the claim that Christianity dominated the slaves' worldview rests on shaky statistical ground at best, even when significant undercounting is taken into consideration.[1]

Recently, this discrepancy between statistical evidence and interpretive emphasis has drawn the attention of religion and slavery historians. In the introductory essay of the *Encyclopedia of African-American Religions,* Larry G. Murphy argues that a complete religious history of African Americans has not been written yet, specifically because the current historiography overwhelmingly focuses on Christianity. Michael A. Gomez and Sylviane A. Diouf both agree with Murphy by pointing out that Islam is a much-neglected aspect of the early African American religious experience. Similarly, John C. Willis reminds historians that nonreligious belief systems are also worthy of study. In "From the Dictates of Pride to the Paths of Righteousness: Slave Honor and Christianity in Antebellum Virginia," Willis suggests that honor often surpassed Christianity as a slave belief system. Finally, Peter Kolchin sums up such criticism of the current historiography of slave religion in his well-received synthesis, *American Slavery, 1619–1877.* Kolchin writes that "historians have recently been so impressed by the force of slave religion that they may well have exaggerated its universality and slighted some of its contradictory implications."[2]

Since antebellum church records do not even begin to support the conclusion that a majority of the slaves converted to Christianity, the current emphasis on this segment of the slave population needs examining. In defense of earlier scholarship, several reasons exist as to why historians might generalize about most slaves converting to Christianity during the antebellum period. The foremost reason is that nineteenth-century sources often suggest such a transformation. For instance, nineteenth-century traveler Thomas Nichols wrote that "[t]he Southern people are eminently religious, and their negroes follow their example." Frederick Law Olmsted, a noted skeptic of the depth and breadth of Christian beliefs within the slave community, went so far as to describe slave participation in and enthusiasm for religious services as "striking and general characteristics." Former Tennessee slave James Thomas even boldly asserted that when traveling among the African Americans of antebellum St. Louis "you won't find an Atheist."[3]

Another explanation for generalizations about Afro-Christianity is that slave and integrated worship services were probably, next to work, the most visible public behavior exhibited by members of the slave population. Therefore, Christian worship services were some of the most documented accounts of individual and collective slave behavior of the antebellum period. Furthermore, given the dramatic differences between many slaves' and their observers' worship styles, these occasions most likely represent the most memorable public slave behavior for those recording their experiences in the Old South. In addition, many antebellum slave narratives were a means to further the abolitionist cause. Authors and publishers sought to conjure feelings of sympathy as well as empathy for the slaves in the hearts and minds of their readers. An example of such an appeal appears in the narrative of Thomas Jones, where the author exclaims, "Oh that all true Christians knew just how the slave feels in view of the religion of this country, by whose sanction men and women are bound, branded, bought and sold!"[4] In writing such lines authors sought to connect their subject and audience via the concept of Christian suffering and thereby draw the reader into their cause. Accordingly, few witnesses, especially those seeking publication for their recollections, could pass up the opportunity to describe their memories of slaves at worship.

Despite these explanations, this chapter's epigraph from an unidentified freedman provides ample evidence for skepticism of such a broad assessment of slave Christianity. The freedman indicates having participated in Christian services and even publicly imitating preachers while he was a slave, yet he did so at the time without a sincere interest in being converted. Furthermore, the former slave admits that Christian slaves considered him "a devil." The speaker's claim that nonbelievers attended slave worship services is reinforced by former slaves Louis Hughes and Thomas Johnson. Hughes recalled that slave prayer meetings "were the joy and comfort of the slaves, and even those who did not profess Christianity were calm and thoughtful while in attendance." As a child, Johnson remembered that "the slaves would sing many religious songs . . . [a]nd I often joined in the singing." It would only be later at the age of sixteen that Johnson "resolved to seek religion."[5] These statements demonstrate that there could be a great disparity between an individual's public participation in worship and his or her acceptance of Christianity. After all, if all slaves in attendance were Christians then who was getting converted or "finding religion" at these meetings? The statements also reveal that Christian slaves distinguished between those whom they considered true believers and mere pretenders. Given the social tensions that demanded extreme discretion between the closest of white and black confidants in the antebellum South, it is not surprising that even the most astute observers of slavery were unaware of the disparity between a slave's public participation in worship services and his or her private belief.

Nonetheless, this does not mean that the division between Christian and non-Christian slaves went undetected. In fact, the identification of Christian and non-Christian elements within the slave community appears in numerous antebellum sources. Frances Kemble hints at such a division when describing the events of an evening walk on the Butler plantation of Georgia. "I went out into the clear starlight to breathe the delicious mildness of the air, and was surprised to hear, rising from one of the houses of the settlement, a hymn sung apparently by a number of voices. The next morning I inquired the meaning of this and was informed that those Negroes on the plantation who were members of the Church were holding a prayer meeting."[6]

Caroline Seabury, a teacher on a Mississippi cotton plantation, reported to her diary that during a festive plantation barbecue she also heard hymns emerging from one of the slave cabins. Upon her further investigation and inquiry, Seabury was informed that the "Christians was havin' meetin'." Allen Parker recalled a similar dichotomy by pointing out that "while the young people were dancing, the old ones would be holding a prayer 'meetin'." Reverend W. H. Robinson described Saturday nights as the time when "the slaves would slip off to church and frolics." Former slave Henry Bibb, in describing Sundays among the slaves, stated that "[t]hose who make no profession of religion, resort to the woods in large numbers on that day to gamble, fight, get drunk, and break the Sabbath." Elizabeth, a former Maryland slave, similarly complained to a slave patrol that while they were breaking up her prayer meeting, "the ungodly are dancing and fiddling till midnight." Elizabeth may have been complaining about the likes of future Bishop M. F. Jamison, who admitted that before his conversion "instead of my enlisting with the Christians, under the leadership of Uncle Chris and O. C. Ola, I followed Eli, the leader of the dances."[7]

Peter Randolph revealed the division between Christian and non-Christian slaves when he described slave funerals. According to Randolph, "If the slave who died was a Christian, the rest of the Christians among them feel very glad, and thank God that brother Charles, or brother Ned, or sister Betsey, is at last free, and gone home to heaven,—where bondage is never known." As with Henry Bibb, Randolph also noted that on Sundays "that portion of them belonging to the church ask of the overseer permission to attend meeting. . . . Others of the slaves, who do not belong to the church, spend their Sabbath in playing with marbles, and other games, for each other's food, &c. Some occupy the time in dancing to the music of a banjo, made out of a large gourd." Fugitive slave John Thompson found the ability to differentiate between Christians and non-Christians useful in his flight to freedom. Upon reaching Washington, DC, he recognized a man "with whom I was acquainted, we having been raised on the same farm." He entrusted the man with his plans for escape and was rewarded with information regarding a safe house. Thompson did so because "I knew this man was a Christian, and therefore that it was safe to trust him, which is not true of all, since there are as many treacherous colored, as white men."[8]

The split between Christians and the "ungodly" was even perceptible among families and larger affiliated groups. Friday Jones described his father as a "desperate wicked man" and noted further that his father's "associates were all wicked." Mary McCray "was the only one in the family who was a Christian," and because her father "was a very wicked man, and her mother was a wicked woman," she spent most of her days "among the old Christians." James Smith recalled that his father lamented on his deathbed that in regard to his children "not one of us professed religion." During the Civil War, Reverend Elijah Marrs found resisting temptation "an up-hill business" because "[i]n the company I belonged to there were only two professed Christians beside myself." Marrs reported that he was not alone in this difficulty, as fellow Christian and African American soldier Swift Johnson complained that "in his company he was the only man who would own Christ." Finally, another former slave, James Williams, attempted to quantify the religious division of a newly arrived group of Alabama slaves when he wrote that "[o]ut of the two hundred and fourteen slaves who were brought out from Virginia, at least a third of them were members of the Methodist and Baptist churches in that State."[9]

Based on the preceding evidence, it is clear that slaves made a definite distinction between those who were Christians and those who were not. In light of the importance that historians assign to the role of Christianity within the slave community, it is equally important to have some understanding of how many slaves were believers. In addition to James Williams's early effort to quantify the number of slave Christians on a given plantation, there is further evidence concerning the approximate proportion and demographic characteristics of Christians and non-Christians within the South's antebellum slave population. The primary means of analysis of this evidence employed here is a quantitative survey of religious data from the Works Progress Administration (WPA) slave narratives and post-1830 slave autobiographies and interviews for all southern slave states with the exception of Delaware.[10] The following questions and categories constituted the survey of these sources.

1. Was the slave/freedperson a Christian while enslaved?
2. If he or she was a Christian during slavery, what was the age at conversion?
3. Did he or she become a Christian following emancipation/attaining freedom?
4. Age at postbellum conversion
5. Sex of slave convert
6. State of birth
7. State of residence when converted (if Christian)
8. Urban or rural slave
9. Occupation (field, house, skilled, other)
10. Did the master(s) allow or prohibit slave worship?
11. Did the master(s) provide access to worship (plantation chapel, etc.)?
12. Did the slave attend independent slave services in the quarters or brush arbors?

Each of these questions provided a measurement of key aspects of the slave religious experience. Questions 1 and 4 produced evidence of whether most slave conversions to Christianity occurred before or after emancipation/freedom and thereby, along with questions 10 and 11, yielded some measure of the effectiveness of the master class's espoused effort to evangelize the slaves. Question 12 quantified the degree of the slaves' independent Christian activities and helped to suggest the extent of the slaves' satisfaction with the form of Christianity whites offered them as well as the degree of slave participation in secret religious proceedings. Questions 2 and 5 helped determine whether a person's age or sex influenced the likelihood of conversion. Questions 6 and 7 measured whether certain regions had unique religious characteristics, such as greater rates of conversion. Finally, questions 8 and 9 revealed whether the work environment of the slave had any special influence on an individual's likelihood to convert.

The information compiled from this survey appears below. Brief explanatory notes or general observations on important findings accompany the data from each question or interrelated group of questions. Explanations for the calculations appear within the notes. At the end of this chapter appear ten tables that accompany text for survey data including multiple categories or detailed comparisons. A synthesis of the findings and a possible interpretation of their meaning follow the completed overviews of the individual data sets.

SURVEY CRITERIA

This survey of slave religious experiences represents an analysis of over four thousand slave narratives, autobiographies, and interviews from 1830 to the mid-twentieth century. These sources, particularly the WPA narratives, are the most significant collection of materials existing for the study of antebellum slave life and, according to Mechal Sobel, are "the richest sources for the social history of Black Christians."[11] The same sources have been used extensively by Albert J. Raboteau, Mechal Sobel, Charles W. Joyner, Eugene D. Genovese, John B. Boles, and Lawrence W. Levine, to name a few highly regarded scholars who address slave religion or culture. Therefore, as these sources inform much of the historiography of slave religion, they are of particular value and interest to this study. However, it is important to note that the overall number of converts surveyed and several particular data sets are small. The data drawn from four thousand slave narratives represent only a tiny portion of the millions of African Americans who languished in bondage. Furthermore, the vast majority of the individuals in these sources were enslaved during and after the 1850s, which means that the breadth of the antebellum era is not evenly represented. It is also true that some states are represented more here than others, given that some states had more narratives written by or collected from former slave residents. More detailed work at the state or local level will be necessary to determine if the overall and regional patterns put forward for consideration apply. As such, the quantitative findings or the interpretations presented here are not in any way considered as definitive, but rather as suggestive of likely or possible general trends. Still, the interpretations do not rest on the quantitative data alone. Numerous primary and secondary sources serve to support the proffered interpretations. It is my hope that the ideas here will be read in the spirit of open inquiry and encourage scholars to think about old questions in new ways.

From the source base described above, 381 individuals provided sufficiently specific conversion data to classify them as either converted or unconverted during their enslavement. For the purposes of this survey, sufficient evidence for conversion or nonconversion depended upon self-identification as a Christian or a non-Christian. Identification as a Christian in this survey did not depend upon an individual being received into any formal or informal church body. For instance, expressions such as "I was converted . . .," "I joined the church . . .," "I became a Christian . . .," or "I got religion . . ." served to identify if and when an individual converted to Christianity. As the Catholic Church does not emphasize the importance of datable conversion experiences, those slaves who did not describe such an event yet continued an antebellum affiliation with the Roman Catholic Church or immediately joined a Protestant denomination when freed, appear as pre-emancipation converts among the survey population. In most cases, though, date-specific conversion data or context clues clearly identified whether an individual converted to Christianity prior to gaining his or her freedom. The case of South Carolinian William Ballard provides a clear-cut example of how non–date-specific information determined an individual's conversion status. "I joined de church when I was 17 years old, because big preaching was going on after freedom for the colored people."[12] In this case, Mr. Ballard obviously did not convert to Christianity until after emancipation and therefore appears as an unconverted individual in the survey data.

As most of the former slaves interviewed by WPA workers were young when enslaved, the survey takes age into account when determining an individual's conversion status. In particular, to prevent skewing survey results by including persons who were too young to convert, I did not use information from unconverted slave children younger than eight in compiling the conversion data. However, child converts younger than eight are represented in the conversion data. While seemingly very young for making such a conscious decision, small children did convert.[13] For instance, former slave Reverend A. J. Stinson of the Colored Methodist Episcopal Church wrote that "[a]t the age of five I was baptized. . . . I then felt my first and lasting impression of religion and realized deeply my obligation as a baptized believer, both to God and to his Church."[14] Likewise, "[a]t age six [southern evangelical minister] Peter Doub attended a camp meeting and was 'considerably impressed with the necessity of serving God.'"[15] The *Quarterly Review of the Methodist Episcopal Church, South* gives additional support to this age criteria in an 1861 article comparing Baptist and Methodist admission standards for children: "The minimum age of those baptized by them [Baptists] is about ten years: few are taken at that age, and fewer still below it. Now in numerous instances there are marked intelligence and piety in children at four and six years of age. Many a child has given every evidence of regeneration at that age."[16] Furthermore, former slave Harry McMillan of Georgia suggested that the youngest slave converts typically joined the church "when they are 10 years old."[17] While the last two quotations indicate that age ten represents a typical experience for many evangelical child conversions, Reverend Stinson and the *Quarterly Review* article also demonstrate that Methodists and Baptists both admitted younger children to the church. This suggests that the range for the earliest evangelical child conversions was four to ten years of age. Seven is the midpoint for this range, but since the Baptists attracted the greatest attention from the slaves, favoring greater maturity in testing for conversion is prudent. Therefore, age eight served as the benchmark for measuring slave conversions among the antebellum South's Protestant denominations.

Conversion data for young people also provide avenues for interpretation beyond the specific individuals interviewed. This is true because "[a]ll human infants are born helpless, dependent on adult care
and adult transmission of their society's culture."[18] Indeed, those who
study child development and family life argue that the nuclear family
is the locus of socialization and that "the central focus of the process
of socialization lies in the internalization of the culture of the society
into which the child is born."[19] Therefore, "[a] child's emergent identity is . . . a snapshot of culture and society."[20] Furthermore, "those
persons who are most interested in religion, who express the strongest need for religion are drawn largely . . . from those groups that
are most concerned to train their members to be religious."[21] Indeed,
many slave Christians would agree with Isaac Williams, who attributed his conversion and work in the ministry to his mother who "inspired [him] every day to labor by the remembrance of her Christian
virtues."[22] This suggests that as children tend to follow the religious
beliefs of their parents, the conversion of young men and women is
also a means of estimating the acceptance of Christianity among older
segments of the slave population.

POPULATION OVERVIEW

The following is a general overview of the demographic characteristics
of the 381 individuals appearing in the conversion survey. Of the 381
individuals surveyed, there are 118 slaves born in the Upper South, 227
born in the Lower South, and 36 of unknown origin. This corresponds
to the Upper South representing 34.2% and the Lower South representing 65.8% of the known survey data.[23] Such proportions closely reflect those of the 1860 United States Census figures, where the Upper
South represented 38.7% and the Lower South 61.3% of the total slave
population.[24] In this survey, the Upper South consists of the states of
Kentucky, Maryland, Missouri, North Carolina, Tennessee, Virginia,
and the District of Columbia while the Lower South comprises Alabama, Arkansas, Florida, Georgia, Louisiana, Mississippi, Oklahoma,
South Carolina, and Texas.

There are 208 males, 169 females, and 4 persons of unknown sex represented in the survey. This translates into males being 55.2% and females being 44.8% of the data for persons with an identifiable sex. The larger proportion of men within the survey reflects the nine-teenth-century reality that male slaves were both more likely to run away and to write a narrative of their slave experiences. Therefore, the male presence within the sources surveyed is greater than it was within the actual slave population. It is important to keep this dis-proportionate male representation in mind when considering survey results, especially for those categories most influenced by sex.

The following age categories reveal the maximum age reached dur-ing slavery for the individuals appearing in the survey data. Children, or those slaves between the ages of 1 to 12, number 117, or 31.8% of the data. Only 8 of the slaves within the Children category are be-low the age of 8. As described in the conversion criteria, all of these are individuals who claimed conversion before reaching their eighth birthday. Therefore, 109 of the 117 individuals in the Children cate-gory were at least eight years of age while enslaved. There are also 117 youths, teenagers between 13 and 18, constituting an identical 31.8% of the slaves surveyed. Adults, classified as anyone nineteen or older, equal 118 or 32.06% of the data. Individuals without specific age clas-sification fall into two additional categories. The category Child-Youth represents slaves whose ages fall somewhere between 1 and 18, while Youth-Adult designates those slaves who were either older teenagers or young adults. In this survey, Child-Youth and Youth-Adult totals are 11 and 5, or 2.99% and 1.35% of the total data. Thirteen individuals were too vague in their self-description to fit within any of the above categories.

CONVERSION DATA

Of the 381 slaves appearing in the survey, 148 indicated that they were Christians during slavery. This figure means that only 38.8% of those surveyed converted to Christianity while they were slaves. In contrast, 233 indicated that they remained unconverted during slavery. A clear majority, 61.2% of the slaves within this survey, were not Christians before gaining their freedom. Even these results are skewed in favor of conversion since this survey actually inflates the number of converts because of the nature of the primary sources. Specifically, individuals appear in the survey data because they provided detailed information about their religious experiences. In fact, only 33 of the 233 persons who were unconverted as slaves either did not indicate conversion or remained unconverted in their description of life after freedom. This indicates that the overwhelming majority of the former slaves in this survey, 348 or 91.3%, were attracted to the message of Christianity at some point in their lives. In other words, those who had little to say about religion, either because of their disinterest or lack of exposure to it, are underrepresented in this study.

In addition to trying to estimate the percentage of Christians within the slave community, this survey examined the influence of geographic location upon conversion. In particular, this study determined the percentage of slave conversions for four geographic regions: Upper South, Lower South, East Coast, and the South and West. The findings from these four categories allow for two major geographical comparisons: Upper to Lower South and the East Coast to the South and West. Of the total number of slave converts, 17 could not be regionally identified.

After adjusting population figures to account for sale and migration to the Lower South, the data revealed that 41 of 105 Upper South slaves converted to Christianity.[25] This translates into 39% of the Upper South slaves surveyed being Christians. Of the 230.5 Lower South slaves, 90, for an identical 39%, converted. This regional equity continues as the number of converts from both the Upper and Lower South closely reflects their share of the survey's total data. Upper South slaves represent 31.3% of the regionally identifiable converts, while those from the Lower South total 68.7%. This demonstrates that the Lower South had almost 3% more converts than their share of the total survey population.

Interestingly, the conversion rates for the older, eastern slave states compared to those for the South and West are strikingly similar to those for the Upper and Lower South.[26] On the East Coast, 57 of 146.5 slaves converted, or 38.9%. Similarly, 74 of 190.5, or 38.8%, of slaves from the South and West converted to Christianity. The consistency of these figures suggests that geography had little bearing on the proportion of Christians among the late antebellum slave population.

SEX

Although males comprise 55.2% of the survey data for persons with an identifiable sex, women slightly outnumber men in regard to the number of converts. Out of 148 slave converts prior to the Civil War, 74 are women, 73 are men, and 1 is of unknown sex. Calculated as a percentage of the converts, women equal 50%, men 49.3%, and unknown 0.7%. Women also led men as to the percentage of their sex who converted as a slave, with 74 of 169 doing so for a total of 43.8%. In comparison, only 35.1%, or 73 of 208 men, converted while enslaved. Based upon this evidence it is clear that women were more likely than men to convert to Christianity as slaves.

It is only in regional comparisons that men outnumber women in regard to the number and percentage of converts. In the Upper South, male converts outnumber female 25 to 16 and represent a larger percentage, 61% to 39%, of the region's slave Christians. However, this may reflect a bias within the primary sources. Again, antebellum slave narratives were typically written by men, of whom a vast majority was from the Upper South. An excellent example of this bias within the primary source material is the state of Maryland. There are 17 males and no females representing the state of Maryland in this survey. Nonetheless, Upper South women still led their male regional counterparts in the percentage of their sex that converted. Only 38.2% of Upper South males converted, while 41.6% of the region's females did so.

In contrast to the Upper South, Lower South women dominated all aspects of conversion in their region. Of the 90 identifiable Lower South converts, 52 are women and 38 are men, for regional percentages of 57.8% and 42.2%. Finally, 45.8% of all Lower South women converted, while only 32.5% of the region's males followed suit. These last two figures represent the highest and lowest conversion percentages for either sex in both regions. Thus, according to this data, Lower South women were the most likely slaves to convert, while Lower South men were the least likely to become Christians.

AGE AT CONVERSION

The survey organized slaves according to their age at conversion using the same categories established for identifying their maximum age in slavery. Of 119 age-identifiable slave Christians, 56, or 47.1%, converted at or before the age of 12. The youth category, those who converted between the ages of 13 and 18, represents 14.3% of the population surveyed. Adult converts equaled 14 in number for a conversion category percentage of 11.8%. Another 30 converts fell into the broader category of Child-Youth, ages 1 to 18, for a 25.2% share of all slave conversions. Only 2, or 1.7%, of the slaves were of the Youth-Adult category. Taken as a whole, these data indicate that the slaves converted at a relatively young age: at least 86.6% of them converted before the age of 18. In fact, only 3 of the age-identifiable converts became a Christian over the age of 25. The average age for those providing a specific age of conversion was 14.[27]

There are some significant differences in conversion age in regard to sex. The most pronounced difference in regard to conversion is that men were much more likely to convert as adults than were women. Almost one-quarter, 23.6%, of male slaves converted as adults. Conversely, only 1 female slave converted after the age of 18. No female slave converted over the age of 25. Furthermore, all but one of the slaves who converted before the age of 8 were women. Therefore, it is clear that slave women tended to convert before slave men, a fact which is supported by comparing their average age of conversion. The average male converted at 15.4 years of age, while women preceded men three years earlier at 12.3 years of age.

SLAVE OCCUPATION

In order to determine whether a slave's assigned duties influenced the prospect for conversion, the survey divided the slaves into five work categories: Field, House, Skilled, Yard, and Other. The Yard category represents young children old enough to perform small tasks around the yard of the big house, such as collecting kindling wood and carrying water to the fields. The Other category is a catchall classification for slaves performing multiple functions and for jobs such as herder and dairy worker that do not fit within the remaining categories. Out of the total survey, 311 former slaves identified their occupations while enslaved. Table 1 outlines each occupation's share of the total known population and breakdown by sex. Table 2 indicates the occupations of those slaves who converted while enslaved. A total of 124 slave converts indicated their occupation during slavery. The data in these two tables suggest there is very little difference between the converts' overall occupations and those of the general survey population. The only major difference between the two groups appears in the Yard category. There were no female converts in that category, which is not surprising since there were only 6 female yard slaves within the entire survey. This absence of female yard slaves thereby inflates the female convert percentage in the Field and House categories as compared to females in the general population. After this discrepancy is taken into consideration, it is obvious that converts strongly resemble the total survey population in regard to occupation and are not over-represented in any specific categories.

Table 3 provides the percentages of slaves within each occupation who converted to Christianity. An "Adjusted Skilled" category appears in this table. This new category combines totals from the "Skilled" category and the number of "Other" slaves that claimed a skill as one of their multiple functions. The "Adjusted Skilled" category measures more precisely whether there was any correlation between skilled labor and an individual's likelihood to convert. The data shown in table 3 indicate that most occupational categories for the general population had similar percentages of converts. Less than seven percentage points separate the conversion percentages for five of the six occupational categories. The two categories with the highest conversion percentages, Other and Adjusted Skilled, while representing occupations with the most independence, are so close to the Field category, the least independent, in conversion percentage that it seems unwise to assign much significance to their highest rank. Ironically, the youngest laborers, yard slaves, were the least likely to convert. While this runs counter to the general trend for conversion, it probably reflects the fact that males, the least likely and oldest slaves to convert, constituted over 71% of the Yard slave category. Furthermore as most slaves began "adult" work by age 12, many would have outgrown the Yard slave category before experiencing conversion.

A gender analysis of occupation and conversion reveals some differences between male and female slaves. Male dominance of the Yard category made it the only occupation in which men led women in con-

version percentage. Males and females also differed as to which occupational categories represent the most and least likely to convert.
Skilled women were the most likely of their sex to convert while female yard slaves were the least likely. In contrast, the Other category
represents the highest occupational conversion percentage for males
with the lowest being for house slaves.

A regional analysis for slave converts demonstrates that there were
some significant differences between the occupations of the Upper and
Lower South slave Christian communities. Table 4 provides the data
supporting this observation.[28] Not surprisingly, occupational data
for regional converts show that field slaves were the largest category
of slave converts in both the Upper and Lower South. However, the
difference between the number of field slaves and the second largest
group, house slaves, was much more pronounced in the Upper South
than in the Lower South. In other words, Upper South Christians were
almost twice as likely to be field slaves as house slaves, whereas Lower
South believers were almost equally represented in each of these categories. These differences reflect the two regions having the opposite
tendencies for conversion in these categories. Using the total occupational conversion percentages from table 3, it is clear that the Upper
South converted a higher percentage of field hands (43.2% to 41.5%)
and a lower percentage of house slaves (30% to 39.4%) than was true
of the general population. The reverse is true for the Lower South.

The final occupational difference between the two regions is that
Upper South Christians were almost twice as likely to be skilled laborers as Lower South converts. However, despite having a higher proportion of skilled laborers among Upper South Christians, the Lower
South converted a larger percentage of its carpenters and blacksmiths.
Clearly, the combination of region and occupation had some impact
on the likelihood of conversion.

RURAL VERSUS URBAN

The survey not only measured regional influence on conversion but
also if where slaves lived within a region influenced the likelihood to
convert. Of primary interest was whether rural or urban slaves were
more likely to become Christians. Table 5 shows the figures related to

this question, revealing that converts were slightly more likely to live in urban areas than the general survey population (14.7% to 10.3%). It also indicates that urban dwellers were much more likely than rural slaves to convert. Nearly 60% of the urban slaves studied were Christians, while less than 40% of their rural brethren were. The increased likelihood for urban slaves to convert is also evident in a comparison of residence and sex.

As shown in table 6, male and female urban slaves led the rural component of their sexes in regard to conversion percentage. In fact, urban females were more than twice as likely as rural women to convert. Although the difference between urban and rural male conversion percentage is much smaller than it is for women, urban males still had a higher conversion percentage than the 35.1% achieved by the total male slave population. Unquestionably, city dwelling increased the possibility for slave conversion regardless of the sex in question. However, neither setting altered the women's position as the most likely sex to convert. Both urban and rural women led their male counterparts in conversion percentage by significant margins.

Whether a slave was more likely to live in a rural or an urban environment depended on his or her location, in the Upper or Lower South. Table 7 presents this statistical evidence and summarizes its influence on conversion. The information from this table reveals that Upper South slaves in the survey were slightly less than four times more likely than Lower South slaves to live in an urban environment (23.1% to 5.8%). Indeed, nearly 95% of the data for Lower South slaves represented rural bondsmen. Accordingly, these regional differences in living environment spilled over into the shape of each region's Christian community. In the Upper South, one-third of the slave Christians lived in urban areas, a proportion well above the category's 10.3% share of the total survey data. In contrast, Lower South Christians overwhelmingly dwelled in rural areas, with fewer than 1 in 10 living in a city. The regional conversion percentages for urban and rural slaves indicate that the Lower South converted a higher total proportion of both categories of slaves (45.6% to 33.3%). However, adding sex to the analysis complicates this uniform picture, with each region alternately assuming the leadership for sex/location-specific·categories. The most interesting finding for the sex/location-specific data is that Upper South rural males were considerably more likely than Upper South rural females to convert (36.5% to 25%). This is the first instance in which males led females in the likelihood to convert.

DID MASTERS ALLOW OR PROVIDE WORSHIP?

The survey attempted to measure the degree of access slaves had to Christian worship. One of the tests for such access was whether or not the slaves indicated that their master(s) either allowed or provided them the opportunity to attend Christian services. This test defined providing worship as masters performing any of the following actions: allowing slaves to attend church with them, reading the Bible to the slaves, instructing slaves by catechism, including slaves in family prayer, hiring an itinerant preacher to hold services, or establishing a plantation chapel.

As evangelicals routinely stressed the powerful influence that attending even one revival could have on the chances for individual conversion, the standard for what constituted being provided with or allowed to worship was low in this survey. For example, if a slave was permitted to attend church with his master only once a year, then his or her master was counted as permitting slaves to and providing them with worship. Furthermore, this survey did not distinguish between masters who allowed slaves to worship only in a controlled setting and those who permitted independent slave services. Therefore, the following data on masters who allowed or provided worship are actually a better measurement for how many slave owners prohibited religion outright or did not actively facilitate worship in any way.

Out of the total survey population, 264 slaves provided sufficient information to classify them as having been allowed to or prohibited from worshiping. Another 228 indicated sufficiently to calculate for the provision of religious instruction. Only 48, or 18.1%, of the slaves were prohibited from having any access to religious services. A larger percentage of masters, 26.8%, made no significant effort to give their slaves religious instruction. Not surprisingly, if the data are recalculated to compare the experiences of the converted to the unconverted, the figures for allowing and providing services change drastically. Converted slaves reported that only 5.34% of their masters prohibited worship and that 10.3% did not offer them any religious instruction. Among the unconverted, 30.8% of masters did not allow the slaves to worship and 41.3% provided no form of Christian services. Clearly, the availability of some form of organized religious instruction played a significant part in the conversion of the slaves.

A regional analysis for the slave owners' approach to Christian religious instruction indicates that the Upper and Lower South differed slightly. The survey data in table 8 show that slave owners from the Upper South were more likely to prohibit and less inclined to provide Christian religious instruction than Lower South masters. Perhaps the fact that Nat Turner's uprising occurred in the Upper South made the region's slaveholders slightly more likely than Lower South masters to prohibit religious instruction. The Upper South's close proximity to free states might also help explain its higher prohibition percentage. In particular, masters might have been leery about slave visions of using the Ohio River to create their own version of the Mosaic Red Sea story.

That Upper South masters were less likely to provide some form of worship for their slaves might reflect their region's greater proportion of urban slaves. As shown in table 9, urban slaves were less likely to be prohibited from worship but were also less likely to be provided with religious instruction by their masters. This difference probably reflects the greater selection that urban slaves had for choosing where to worship. As cities provided more opportunities for worship, urban masters usually did not have to provide religious instruction in order for their slaves to have access to it. Likewise, the slaves' easy access to religious services in cities also helps explain why urban masters were less likely to prohibit worship than rural masters. Specifically, the ease with which urban slaves could find worship, coupled with the shorter travel distances for church, probably made prohibition of religious instruction so difficult to enforce as well as less objectionable that fewer masters attempted such a policy.

INDEPENDENT SLAVE WORSHIP

Independent slave worship, explored in table 10, is the final category of analysis drawn from the survey data. Table 10 demonstrates how many of the surveyed population indicated that they did or did not participate in independent African American worship services. In addition, the data reveal some of the personal characteristics of those who did attend unsanctioned prayer meetings and covert brush arbor gatherings. In most cases, an indication that an individual had never attended any form of worship prior to freedom provided the standard for determining those who did not attend independent worship services. The use of this standard once again reflects the survey's dependence on the information (or lack thereof) in the sources. Accordingly, this standard undoubtedly excludes additional slaves who did not attend and therefore logically did not discuss their lack of attendance at these services.

The data from the survey population indicate that only a small percentage of the slaves participated in exclusively African American worship services. In fact, only 23 of 148, or 15.5%, of Christians described having attended independent prayer meetings or brush arbor gatherings. As independent worship services are one of the most significant pieces of evidence for the depth of Christianity within the slave community, a larger sampling of religious evidence seems necessary to confirm this finding. Accordingly, I reexamined note entries for 1,624 former slaves covered by this survey. Of these individuals, only 169, or 10.4%, indicated that they personally attended such services. This suggests that while many former slaves knew that these services existed, few actually attended.[29] That no greater than 15.5% of slaves attended independent worship services really should not be surprising. In the wake of Nat Turner's rebellion, these services were often held despite their explicit prohibition by state law or slave owner mandate. Therefore, slaves participating in these meetings did so at the risk of harassment or injury from slave patrols or angry plantation authority figures.[30]

That most of the admitted participants were women is also not surprising given the previous evidence for conversion and sex. However, the fact that virtually half of those attending independent and covert services did not convert prior to freedom is intriguing. Most likely these unconverted participants were prospective converts invited by a concerned Christian friend or relative. On the other hand, perhaps the idea of defying one's master or simple curiosity drew unbelieving slaves to these black-only gatherings. In either case, this evidence reinforces the need for scholars to separate the slaves' participation in worship from actual belief. Again, this is particularly true in this case since historians frequently use clandestine services as evidence for asserting the depth of Christianity within the slave population.

CONCLUSIONS

For generations, antebellum Afro-Christianity has drawn detailed commentary from its observers and attracted the enthusiastic attention of scholars. The reasons for this fascination are myriad. For slaveholders, Afro-Christianity imbued their social structure with a missionary hue and validated their belief in slavery as a divinely sanctioned, civilizing institution. Abolitionists viewed slave Christians both as evidence of the common humanity of mankind and as showing the degrading influence of human bondage. Similarly, African American Christian worship captivated nineteenth-century travelers as an exotic outgrowth of the South's peculiar institution and as a marketable tale to tell.

Historians from the twentieth century were likewise intrigued with antebellum Afro-Christianity. From Melville J. Herskovitz to John W. Blassingame, Afro-Christianity served as a means of asserting African American humanity and agency within the dehumanizing confines of slavery. In fact, Afro-Christianity has at times meant all things to a wide number of thoughtful scholars, especially as a tool to dismantle the arguments of Ulrich B. Phillips and Stanley M. Elkins.[31] To Herskovitz and Sobel, Afro-Christianity demonstrates the vitality of African traditions despite the racist, conformist pressures of American society. For Lawrence W. Levine and Charles W. Joyner, slave Christians reveal the triumph of African American cultural creativity over the stagnating influences of forced labor and physical deprivation. Finally, Eugene D. Genovese and John W. Blassingame use Afro-Christianity to assert the slaves' sense of community and personal resistance against the onslaught of white oppression.

The evidence behind these scholars' interpretations leaves little doubt that Afro-Christianity did represent a significant achievement of and was a sustaining influence for its believers. However, therein lies the rub. This quantitative survey of slave religious experiences suggests that fewer slaves became Christians than we have traditionally believed. At best, almost four out of ten slaves in the survey identified themselves as Christians during the late antebellum era. But given the bias in the primary sources available, the survey would suggest that it is more likely that fewer than three in ten slaves of the surveyed slaves embraced Christianity. These findings allow for at least some reevaluation of the role of Christianity within the slave community. A closer look at evangelical Protestantism and the evidence used to describe elements of Afro-Christianity helps support this interpretation.

Despite its many communal manifestations, Christianity is at its core a highly individualistic religion. Either one believes the tenets of faith and applies them to one's life or one does not. This is especially true of evangelical Protestantism, the dominant form of Christianity within the southern slave population. Evangelical Protestantism requires that its practitioners demonstrate a datable, individual, and life-changing conversion experience. In other words, according to evangelical Protestants, Christian salvation rests solely on an individual's personal relationship with God.

That many individuals, even those with pious families, resisted or refused to make that personal commitment to Christian living is clear. For instance, in 1862, minister's wife and slave owner Mary Jones wrote to her son about her concern for the soul of a gravely ill slave named Joe: "Yesterday afternoon I walked over to see him . . . and had a conversation with him about the state of his soul. He said it would have been better for him if he had thought more about it now." Mary Jones wrote that Joe's answer surprised and worried her because "for three years he had been a constant and an attentive attendant upon our Sabbath night school, where I had often spoken to him of our Savior." Likewise, Alice Green of Georgia resisted her mother and sisters' pleas to become a Christian until she was free and over seventy years old. Ed McCree and Joe Rollins proved even more resistant to the Christian message. McCree told WPA interviewers that "I ain't never jined up wid no church. I ain't got no reason why, only I jus' ain't never had no urge from inside of me to jine." Likewise, Rollins exclaimed that "[a]ll what wants to ought to have 'ligion. I don't never fool along wid it." Finally, Paul Smith described slave religious apathy on a broader scale by pointing out that "[s]ome of dem slaves never wanted no 'ligion, and dey jus' laughed at us cause us testified and shouted."[32] While identifying the forces that created such resistance to Christianity is important, for the purposes of this discussion it is sufficient to say that the presence of a strong Christian core within the slave population did not translate into anything approaching universal acceptance of their beliefs or participation in their activities.

As described earlier, the rejection of Christianity by many slaves created a definite, detectable division between slave Christians and their fellow bondsmen. For instance, Cornelius Garner of Virginia noted that "we could go to church if we wanted to. Some few went but de biggest part of us jes stayed 'round de house and slept and talked." Elaborating further, Garner said, "[d]e Christians had dere 'fairs on one farm an' de sinners had dere frolics on 'nother farm." Georgia slave, Uncle Willis recalled that "[c]hurch people would have singin' and prayin' and de wicked people would have dancin' and singin.'" Louis Napoleon expressed a similar sentiment by remembering how "[t]he wicked slaves expended their pent up emotions in song and dance" while "the religious among [the slaves] would gather at one of the cabin doors and give thanks to God." W. H. Robinson detected this division among slaves awaiting sale in a slave trader's pen. "[W]e went back to the negro trader's pen, but before we got there we heard singing of two classes. Some religious songs, such as 'God has delivered Daniel,' and other melodies, while others were singing the songs of the world, all seemingly rejoicing in their own way." Frederick Douglass recalled that during the Christmas holidays "[t]he staid, sober, thinking and industrious . . . would employ themselves in making cornbrooms, mats, horse-collars, and baskets . . . [while] the larger part engaged in such sports and merriments as playing ball, wrestling, running footraces, fiddling, dancing, and drinking whiskey." Douglass even indicated that the staid and sober were a clear minority by declaring that "[t]he most of us used to drink it down . . . [as] [w]e felt . . . that we had almost as well be slaves to man as to rum."[33] These are but a few of the more obvious statements from former slaves indicating a clear division between Christians and nonbelievers.

That most of the preceding statements focus on singing and dancing as non-Christian behavior is extremely significant since these two activities are well documented, common aspects of antebellum slave culture. In fact, scholars such as Roger D. Abrahams and Lawrence W.

Levine have written extensively about how African American singing and dancing at events like corn huskings were an important, widespread outlet of cultural expression and personal joy for the slaves.[34] However, Christian African Americans consistently identify secular songs and dancing as unacceptable behavior that they abandoned once converted. For instance, Marie Clements noted, "I danced till I joined the church," while South Carolinian George McAlilley recalled, "I didn't jine de church in slavery time; lak to dance then." Hector Smith pointed out the sinful nature of secular music when he said, "I put all dem other kind of songs away when I is change to a better way of livin." Finally, Joseph Holmes and Siney Bonner offer statements that suggest that most Christians had to avoid attending plantation celebrations. Holmes states that "[i]n days gone by I went to plenty of dances an' candy pullins but I doesn't do dat any mo.' I's a preacher." Similarly Bonner points out that the Baptists would "[t]urn you out sho' if you drink too much cawn licker, or dance."[35] Clearly, the drinking, singing, and dancing that Roger D. Abrahams's work shows were common at these "frolics" were activities for Christians to avoid. Indeed, Caroline Seabury's account of slave Christians holding a prayer meeting during a plantation barbecue demonstrates that Christians did separate themselves from these prohibited activities when possible. Harriet Beecher Stowe even noted the importance of this distinction on a Florida plantation in 1879. According to Stowe, "It appears that dancing is selected as the one thing to be given up when the postulant thinks of joining the church. . . . [I]n their view this was the one sign of self surrender, and the violin, as the excitement to dancing, was therefore held as a profane thing in divine worship."[36] Therefore, given the ubiquity of secular singing and dancing throughout the slave narratives and their consistent condemnation by Christians, the reality of a majority Afro-Christian community seems problematic.

Additional evidence for a smaller Christian community among the slaves exists in the description of independent worship services. Most slaves were not permitted to hold independent worship services, and therefore a majority of these gatherings were clandestine. In most cases, these meetings required participants to slip off into the woods undetected or to gather secretly in a single cabin. Such procedures are significant in light of the fact that over 70 percent of all slave owners possessed fewer than ten slaves and that one-half of all slaves lived on farms of twenty or fewer slaves. The vast majority of these slaves either lived in the same house with their masters or in very close proximity to them. Given this proximity of master and slave in these settings, it is unlikely that regular, unsanctioned worship services would go un-noticed. Indeed, the very notion that the Christian core was an "invis-ible institution" suggests that the slave church was small. It would be extremely difficult to conceal a large, frequently meeting, and vibrant body of worshipers in the Old South. Therefore, the very prerequisites for clandestine meetings likely precluded half of all slaves from at-tending or holding such services on a regular basis even if they desired to do so.[37]

Testimony from slaves like Louis Napoleon also provides evidence for a smaller slave Christian community. Like many other informants, Napoleon indicates that the slaves "would gather at one of the cabin doors and give thanks to God."[38] That the slaves usually gathered in a single cabin suggests that the number of people attending was small. This is true because the typical antebellum slave cabin measured ap-proximately sixteen by eighteen feet.[39] It is difficult to imagine fitting a large number of people, in addition to those already living there, in such close quarters. This is particularly true given some of the descrip-tions of animated worship that transpired at these gatherings. While it is impossible to establish a definitive figure for typical attendance at cabin prayer meetings, the recollections of Louisiana slave Charlotte Brooks seem to suggest a reasonable figure for a cabin worship service given the space considerations. Brooks recalled that she and twelve other adult slaves regularly gathered for clandestine prayer meetings on the sugar plantation where she lived.[40] As Louisiana sugar planta-tions were usually quite large, Brooks's estimate also fits well with the evidence for only 10 to 15 percent of all slaves actually attending for-bidden worship.

Another characteristic of independent slave worship that supports the argument for a smaller Christian community is that these meet-ings were, in most cases, forbidden. While prayer meetings occurred despite this prohibition, the survey conducted for this study and the slave narratives both confirm that at least some masters succeeded in denying their slaves any contact with Christianity. The survey revealed that almost one in five masters prohibited all religious instruction and more than one in four made no effort to offer Christianity to their slaves. The testimony from numerous former slaves demonstrates that the restrictions and apathy of at least some of these masters successfully kept their bondsmen from coming into contact with Christianity. Ophelia Whitney of North Carolina stated that "[w]e warn't teached nothin,' not even religion." Missourian William Nelson goes even further by claiming, "I neber heard of no 'ligion, baptizing, nor God, nor Heaven, de Bible nor education down on de plantashun." Finally, Virginian Henry Banks remarked that "I did not hear a sermon preached during the time I lived with S——, there was no meeting for us to go to. . . . At this place there was no colored minister—there were no Christian people on that place. I never heard any religious songs while I was there."[41]

Prohibition aside, many slaves, as well as many whites, simply had little to no familiarity with Christianity because of their geographical isolation within the vast and rapidly expanding territory of the United States. In 1850, the *Alabama Baptist Advocate* lamented this fact in the article "Destitution of Religious Knowledge":

> That there is a great destitution of religious knowledge—"a famine of the word of the Lord"—in many portions of our country, South and West cannot be denied. Our ministry are too few to supply the wants of our extended and increasing territory. Comparatively few of our churches are supplied with more than monthly preaching, while vast numbers of them have not even that—to say nothing of the wide fields wherein as yet no churches have been planted. In this state of things, it can be imagined that a most lamentable want of instruction . . . prevails in many parts of the country.[42]

Eight years later in an address on domestic missions, the Methodist Episcopal Church, South, would offer a very similar assessment of the southern population's access to religious instruction: "It is found, upon close examination, that in all the Conferences there are numerous tracts of country, sparsely settled, which are without the regular ministrations of the gospel: there are few, if any houses of worship, and the people are either too poor to pay for the gospel of Christ, or have never learned to value the instructions of Christianity. It is a lamentable fact that many of these communities are to be found in our oldest States and within the geographical limits of long-established and numerically strong Conferences."[43]

An 1849 report by Baptist missionary James E. Sharp gives specific mention of his embryonic efforts in a region fitting this description. Reverend Sharp identified the region, dubbed Africa, as a place in the interior of Georgia where "[n]ot more than one half the inhabitants hear preaching once in the year."[44] It was locations such as "Africa" that led the Alabama Baptist State Convention of 1850 to estimate that in the South "[o]nly about one-tenth of our population, according to a most liberal charity, can be regarded as pious."[45] Obviously, many mid-nineteenth-century southerners of all races had little to no access to Christian instruction. Therefore, based on the evidence from both the Baptist and Methodist churches, it is not difficult to imagine scenarios where non-Christian master and slave, living in plantation or upcountry isolation, remained untouched by the Second Great Awakening and felt little, if any, influence of Christianity on their lives. Such circumstances are hardly a ringing endorsement for interpreting the nearly universal acceptance of Christianity within the South's white, much less slave, population.

There is substantial evidence to suggest that historians have overestimated the size of the slave Christian community. Even this study's survey, indicating that 38.8% of the slaves converted to Christianity, inflates the believer population due to the nature of the primary sources available. Perhaps a more likely figure for the percentage of slave converts appears in an essay by historian John C. Willis. Willis uses a Virginia planter's religious survey of his slaves to argue that 25% of the slaves were probably Christians. This seems to be a reasonable midpoint between the inflated findings of this survey and the 14.3% of churched blacks that Mechal Sobel describes as "very far from accurate." A figure of 25% also squares with Albert J. Raboteau's figure of 2.7 million church members out of a late nineteenth-century African American population of 8.3 million. Raboteau argues that "[t]his astounding figure sheds some light on the extent to which slaves had adopted Christianity in the antebellum South."[46] However, in light of this study, Raboteau's figure of 32.5% for late nineteenth-century African American church membership also makes sense as the result of a rising tide of Christian conversions emerging from the Civil War. Specifically, freedmen, remembering the Christian core's identification with the ancient Israelites, viewed emancipation as evidence of God's power and flocked to the Church in record numbers.

In addition to questioning the historiographical emphasis on slave Christianity, the survey presented in this study also provides insight on the characteristics of what may be called the slave Christian core. In particular, the survey offers information on how sex, age, occupation, region, and urban or rural residence affected an individual's likelihood to convert to Christianity. Some of the findings may not be new or surprising, but several may be novel, and all help provide greater detail on the general characteristics of the slave Christian community.

In regard to sex differences, the survey of slave religious experiences confirmed what many historians have stated about women and southern religion: women were the majority of the region's Christians.[47] The survey supported this interpretation in two specific ways. First of all, slave women represented 50% of all converts despite comprising less than 45% of the survey population. Second, a significantly higher percentage of women, 43.8%, converted than men, 35.1%. Thus, women were not only more likely to convert but also represented a share of the convert population larger than their share of the total survey population.

While the survey results for sex were not surprising, the findings for age and conversion do raise an interesting question. Was the Christian core of the slave community predominantly young or was it made up of older individuals? Older slaves clearly held a special position as elders among the religious slaves. This fact made older slave Christians highly visible and more frequently mentioned within the historical record. Additionally, John C. Willis offers a logical argument that fear of approaching death made many older slaves convert, thus giving the Christian core a more mature membership.[48] However, census data from 1860 and the survey results for age at conversion complicate this interpretation.

According to the United States Census, 74.3%, or 2,915,002, of 3,924,460 age-identifiable slaves were under age 30 in 1860. Furthermore, only 570,925, or 14.4%, of age-identifiable slaves were older than

40.[49] Thus the slave population was overwhelmingly young, with relatively few slaves living to see their fortieth birthday. The survey results complement these figures by showing that the average slave Christian converted as a teen and that nearly all converted before age 25. Therefore, assuming that most of these converts did not live to an advanced age, we can surmise that most slave Christians were young.

The interpretation for a young slave Christian core also makes sense in terms of the mid-nineteenth-century efforts to convert slaves to Christianity. Evangelical Christian literature consistently hammers home the idea that the older an individual is, the less likely he or she is to convert. An article from 1856 on the religious training of children presents a familiar argument on this subject. "Daily observation shows that as men grow older, they become more hardened in sin, less and less pervious to conviction—with a constantly increasing indifference to their obligations to God."[50] Although they did not stop proselytizing adults, evangelicals were led by such thinking to focus a significant amount of energy on bringing children into the church through the use of Sunday schools and catechisms. That these efforts bore fruit among the slaves is clear. For instance, a Louisiana Presbyterian praises the results of "three oral Sabbath Schools . . . of near 50 colored children, who are learning to recite our catechism very rapidly."[51] Baptist slave Lucy Skipwith described equally successful results in a letter to her master, John Hartwell Cocke. "I am rejoiced to tell you that we have had a most beautiful revival of religion amongst us. . . . [W]e [sic] have 11 that has been converted within the last two weeks. There is not a grown person among them, they are all my Sabbath School Schollars [sic]."[52] In 1852, overseer Jonathan Roberson reported to his employer George Noble Jones that "forty one of your negroes [were] baptized last Sunday in the Canall [sic]. . . . Davy and Polly and all the young set."[53] Given the instructional emphasis placed upon children and the fact that organized efforts to convert the slaves began in 1829, only thirty-two years before the Civil War, that a majority of the Christian core was young seems plausible. On the other hand, if the sources that emphasize the presence of older slaves at Christian worship are accurate, then this is yet another indication that the number of slave Christians was smaller than most scholars believe since older slaves comprised less than 15 percent of the enslaved population.

The data for slave occupation and conversion demonstrated that the Christian core closely resembled the general survey population in regard to their distribution among the five occupational categories. The survey results also did not indicate any apparent link between a slave's occupation and his or her likelihood to convert. These findings contradict the belief of nineteenth-century Presbyterian minister Charles Colcock Jones that house slaves were more likely to convert than those of other occupations.[54] In fact, only when I analyzed how sex or region affected occupational conversion percentages did significant differences emerge between the categories. However, while conversion differences are apparent for slaves of a certain sex or region, there was little consistent evidence in the narratives and autobiographies to offer an interpretation for these results. Based upon the evidence presented here, all that is certain is that slave Christians appear to have been no more likely to work in a specific occupation than other slaves.

In contrast to the findings for occupation, the data for slave residence and conversion are both more conclusive and more significant. This survey suggests that urban or rural residence was more important to an individual's likelihood to convert than was living in either the Upper or Lower South. More specifically, the findings presented here indicate that by the late antebellum period, there was no difference between the percentage of slaves who converted in the Upper and Lower South. An additional comparison between the slave states of the East Coast and those of the South and West yielded the same result, as roughly 39% of these slaves also converted to Christianity. These findings suggest that by the late antebellum period, region was not a very significant factor in determining slave conversion. In contrast, urban slaves were much more likely to convert than were their rural brethren. Only 38% of rural slaves in the survey converted to Christianity before freedom, while 56.8% of urban slaves did. This pattern of urban slaves converting at a higher percentage than rural slaves even remains true when sex and region are added as categories of analysis.

The findings for cities largely reflect the urban slaves' greater access to and relatively greater independence in practicing the Christian faith. Many evangelicals recognized that cities had greater numbers of white and black conversions and directed their "greatest energies" to these "large multitude[s] of immortal beings."[55] Perhaps many evangelicals even felt that the larger number of converts had divine sanction. For instance, in 1855 the Baptist *Home and Foreign Journal* pointed out that "Our Lord and his apostles directed their labors towards towns and cities; and it is a fact, which a trial of the past two years has abundantly verified, that missionary labor in those places succeed better, and yields larger results, than the same amount of labor does in the country. While therefore we should not neglect the country, we should provide promptly for towns and cities."[56] As a result of this urban focus, in 1860 nearly half of the denomination's sixty-nine domestic missionaries held assignments in cities. This is a surprisingly large proportion given the South's overwhelmingly rural population. Understandably, such an emphasis on cities and towns greatly increased an urban slave's possibilities for worship and therefore likelihood to convert.

On the other hand, the steady southwesterly migration of nineteenth-century masters and slaves is the most logical reason for the equal percentage of slave converts between the various regions of the South. As Christian masters and slaves moved from the Upper South and East to the fertile, newly opened lands of the Lower South and West, they carried their faith with them. According to Sylvia R. Frey and Betty Wood, "Despite the social dislocation and the religious disarray caused by forced migration, black migrants [from the Upper South] stamped their own religious identity on the landscape of the developing West."[57] In this way, the evangelical expansion that began with the Cane Ridge, Kentucky, revival of 1801 spread outward into many of the newly settled areas of the South. By 1860, this migration fused with the Second Great Awakening to create a regional religious culture that yielded similar conversion patterns among the slaves it reached.[58]

That the migration of Upper South and eastern slaves did affect the religious experiences of many African Americans in the Lower South and West is evident from the testimony of their fellow slaves and the ministers who served them. For example, Alabama slave James Williams noted that one-third of the new slaves on his plantation were Methodists and Baptists from Virginia.[59] The life of Charlotte Brooks testifies to the influence that such migrants could have on their new environment. Despite being denied access to church services, Brooks stated that she converted to Christianity under the guidance of a Virginia-born Christian living in Louisiana.[60] Other new slave arrivals managed to effect change on an even wider scale. For instance, Reverend Edwin Cook of Mississippi recalled that former South Carolina slaves living on a plantation near Vicksburg "applied to [their owner] for a Methodist preacher to be sent to them as many were of that church, and all had been accustomed to hearing preaching from Methodist preachers in the state whence they had come." The planter promptly secured a missionary to serve his plantation's religious needs.[61] Virginia slaves are even credited for reviving the previously dissolved First African Baptist Church of New Orleans in 1834.[62] In this way, migration minimized the religious differences between older settled regions and newer ones by transplanting values and beliefs along with the people.

Even considering the religiously homogenizing influence that massive migration had on many southerners, the late antebellum balance between Upper and Lower South slave conversions still may be surprising to some. In part this is a natural reaction to the Upper South's reputation for better slave treatment. However, as Eugene D. Genovese shows that the treatment of small farm slaves in the Upper South was "about the same" as that of Lower South plantation slaves, such doubts are based on a false assumption.[63] On the other hand, the Upper South's reputation for having a more Christian slave community partly rests on the greater number of churches within the region as compared to the Lower South. Indeed, a statistical comparison of the two regions' religious institutions reveals great differences between the Upper and Lower South. Upper South counties with the highest percentages of slaves as a share of the total population averaged 15,599 persons and 29 churches containing 9,461 seats per county in 1860. This meant that 60% of the population in the Upper South's heaviest slave-owning counties could be offered a seat in church every Sunday morning. In contrast, Lower South states averaged 14,520 residents and 19 churches with 5,947 seats per county in 1860. This meant that despite similar population figures, only 42% of the people in the Lower South's heaviest slave-owning counties were guaranteed morning access to a church pew.[64] However, while these statistics show that the Upper South led in church accommodations, they ignore the Lower South's leading role in sending missionaries to the slaves.

By 1860 southern Methodists had established eighty missions to the slaves in the Upper South while operating 249 in the Lower South. The Southern Baptist Convention sent twenty-two domestic missionaries to the Upper South in 1860 while committing forty-two to the Lower South.[65] Furthermore, two of the most influential activists for sending missions to the slaves, William Capers, a Methodist, and Charles Colcock Jones, a Presbyterian, lived and worked as missionaries in the Lower South. Numerous articles in antebellum periodicals reflect their and other Lower South Christians' significant leadership roles in ministering to the slaves. For example, leading religious journals featured the missionary work of Capers and Jones in South Carolina and Georgia as models for converting African Americans.[66] The North Carolina Baptist newspaper, the *Biblical Recorder,* used a circular letter written by the Bethel Baptist Association of Alabama to encourage their readers to offer their slaves greater access to religious instruction.[67] Finally, in 1844 the Synod of Kentucky credited Georgia Presbyterians with inspiring them to pursue the conversion of the Commonwealth's slaves more vigorously.[68] Therefore, based on the significantly greater presence and influence of slave missions in the Lower South, it is not unreasonable to suggest that the two regions had reached conversion parity by 1860 despite the clear difference in regard to the number of churches.

Another factor supporting the erroneous idea that the Upper South contained more slave Christians is the disproportionate coverage that large urban churches have received in the literature of slave religion. As the majority of these urban congregations were located in the Upper South, it is easy to get the impression that Upper South slaves were more likely to be Christians due to the presence of these dynamic, African American–dominated institutions. This is particularly true because most of the coverage on these churches is not part of a systematic analysis of conversion. Instead, the focus on urban churches usually reflects the historian's desire to demonstrate the slaves' ability to carve out areas of personal freedom within the institution of slavery. For instance, in *Slave Religion,* Albert J. Raboteau describes separate black churches as significant areas of "institutional freedom and self-governance for slaves." Raboteau then proceeds to describe the large African American churches of Williamsburg, Richmond, Petersburg, Savannah, Huntsville, Mobile, Natchez, New Orleans, Louisville, Lexington, Georgetown, St. Louis, Nashville, Baltimore, and Charleston.[69]

While these churches represent important achievements, they are hardly characteristic of the religious experiences of the vast majority of slaves. Former slave Charles Octavius Boothe even questioned the overall significance of these churches in his late nineteenth-century study of African American Baptists in Alabama: "True, there were a few colored churches in 'slavery time,' three missionary and one primitive, but what were three churches in the midst of such a vast population, scattered over so much territory?"[70] Indeed, most slave Christians would have worshiped in an integrated rural church where their level of participation within religious services depended solely upon the congregation's white members. Thus, while attempting to refute the arguments of U. B. Phillips and Stanley M. Elkins, historians unintentionally fuel two major misconceptions about slave religion by focusing on these atypical churches. First, historians have created the illusion of greater slave Christianity in the Upper South than actually existed. Second, urban slaves represented only a tiny portion of the overall slave population. By giving so much attention to urban churches, historians overemphasize the locations with the highest concentrations of slave Christians and the highest rates of conversion. In doing so, scholars have used unrepresentative examples to support the generalization that most slaves were Christians and have perhaps overstated the case.

The findings of this survey raise questions about many of the current arguments concerning the breadth of slave Christianity in the antebellum South. The most important issue raised here is the proposition that most slaves did not accept Christianity as their belief system. This interpretation rests on a detailed survey of slave religious experiences in which less than 40 percent of the slaves identified themselves as Christians. Given these findings, it might be more appropriate to say that a small, strong, and visible Christian core existed within the southern slave population. Furthermore, this Christian core appears as a detectable division within the slave community, with women, the young, and urban dwellers being disproportionately associated with this body of believers.

TABLE 1. Known Occupations of Slaves in Survey

	FIELD	HOUSE	SKILLED	YARD	OTHER
Male	91	27	20	15	20
Female	44	67	2	6	19
Total of known occupations	135	94	22	21	39
% of known occupations	43.4%	30.2%	7.1%	6.8%	12.5%
% Male	67.4%	28.7%	90.9%	71.4%	51.3%
% Female	32.6%	71.3%	9.1%	28.6%	48.7%
% of males in occupation	52.6%	15.6%	11.6%	8.7%	11.6%
% of females in occupation	31.9%	48.6%	1.4%	4.3%	13.8%

TABLE 2. Occupations of Slave Converts

	FIELD	HOUSE	SKILLED	YARD	OTHER
Male	31	7	8	4	9
Female	25	30	1	0	9
Total of known occupations	56	37	9	4	18
% of known occupations	45.2%	29.8%	7.3%	3.2%	14.5%
% Male	55.4%	18.9%	88.9%	100.0%	50.0%
% Female	44.6%	81.1%	11.1%	0.0%	50.0%
% of males in occupation	52.5%	11.9%	13.6%	6.8%	15.3%
% of females in occupation	38.5%	46.2%	1.5%	0.0%	13.8%

TABLE 3. Percentage of Converts per Occupation

	FIELD	HOUSE	SKILLED	YARD	OTHER	ADJUSTED SKILL
Male converts	31	7	8	4	9	8
Female converts	25	30	1	0	9	3
Total converts	56	37	9	4	18	11
Males in occupation	91	27	20	15	20	21
Females in occupation	44	67	2	6	19	4
Total in occupation	135	94	22	21	39	25
% of occupation converted	41.5%	39.4%	40.9%	19.0%	46.2%	44.0%
% of males converted	34.1%	25.9%	40.0%	26.7%	45.0%	38.1%
% of females converted	56.8%	44.8%	50.0%	0.0%	47.4%	75.0%

TABLE 4. Occupations of Slaves and Slave Converts by Region

	FIELD	HOUSE	SKILLED	YARD	OTHER
Upper South converts	16	9	4	1	4
% of Upper South converts	47.1%	26.5%	11.8%	2.9%	11.8%
Total Upper South	37	30	11	6	11
% Upper South converted	43.2%	30.0%	36.4%	16.7%	36.4%
Lower South converts	30	27	5	3	12
% of Lower South converts	39.0%	35.1%	6.5%	3.9%	15.6%
Total Lower South	82	59	11	13	26
% Lower South converted	36.6%	45.8%	45.5%	23.1%	46.2%

TABLE 5. Rural and Urban Slaves and Slave Converts

	RURAL	URBAN
Total in survey	321	37
% of survey	89.7%	10.3%
Converts	122	21
% of converts	85.3%	14.7%
% of rural and urban converted	38.0%	56.8%

TABLE 6. Rural and Urban Slave Converts by Sex

	RURAL		URBAN	
	Male	Female	Male	Female
Total in survey	181	139	22	15
Converted	63	59	8	13
% converted	34.8%	42.4%	36.4%	86.7%

TABLE 7. Regional Urban and Slave Population

	RURAL			URBAN		
	Male	Female	Total Rural	Male	Female	Total Urban
Upper South	52	28	80	15	9	24
% of region			76.9%			23.1%
Converts	19	7	26	5	8	13
% converted	36.5%	25.0%	33.3%	33.3%	88.9%	54.2%
% of Upper South converts			66.7%			33.3%

	RURAL			URBAN		
	Male	Female	Total Rural	Male	Female	Total Urban
Lower South	108	103	211	7	6	13
% of region			94.2%			5.8%
Converts	35	47	82	3	5	8
% converted	32.4%	45.6%	45.6%	42.9%	83.3%	61.5%
% of Lower South converts			91.1%			8.9%

TABLE 8. Religious Instruction by Region

UPPER SOUTH	NOT ALLOWED	%	NOT PROVIDED	%	ALLOWED	PROVIDED
Converts	2	5.0%	4	15.4%	38	22
Unconverted	14	35.9%	17	51.5%	25	16
Total	16	20.3%	21	35.6%	63	38
LOWER SOUTH	NOT ALLOWED	%	NOT PROVIDED	%	ALLOWED	PROVIDED
Converts	4	4.6%	6	8.0%	83	69
Unconverted	26	29.5%	31	38.3%	62	50
Total	30	17.1%	37	23.7%	145	119

TABLE 9. Religious Instruction for Urban and Rural Slaves

RURAL SOUTH	NOT ALLOWED	%	NOT PROVIDED	%	ALLOWED	PROVIDED
Converts	5	4.7%	7	7.6%	102	85
Unconverted	37	29.6%	46	40.0%	88	69
Total	42	18.1%	53	25.6%	190	154
URBAN SOUTH	NOT ALLOWED	%	NOT PROVIDED	%	ALLOWED	PROVIDED
Converts	1	5.9%	3	27.3%	16	8
Unconverted	2	25.0%	2	40.0%	6	3
Total	3	12.0%	5	31.2%	22	11

TABLE 10. Independent Slave Worship

	ATTENDED	% OF TOTAL	DID NOT ATTEND	% OF TOTAL	CONVERTS ATTENDED	% OF ATTENDING	UNCONVERTED ATTENDED	% OF ATTENDING
Male	18	40.0%	18	58.1%	9	20.0%	9	20.0%
Female	27	60.0%	13	41.9%	14	31.1%	13	28.9%
Total	45		31		23	51.1%	22	48.9%
% of Survey	11.8%		8.1%					

2

CHRIST IN CHAINS

Slaves, obey your earthly masters with respect and fear, and with sincerity of heart, just as you would obey Christ.
—EPHESIANS 6:5

Church was what they called it but all that preacher talked about was for us slaves to obey our masters and not to lie and steal. Nothing about Jesus was ever said and the overseer stood there to see the preacher talked as he wanted him to talk.
—CHARLIE VAN DYKE, North Carolina slave, in Rawick, *American Slave*

In the words of Charles W. Joyner, slave Christianity gave African Americans "a source of strength and endurance that enabled them to triumph over the collective tragedy of enslavement." Such words are typical of the way that most historians use Afro-Christianity to counter the argument that slavery stripped Africans of their culture and reduced them to an infantile state of existence. This defense of African American spiritual vitality even suggests that no master-imposed boundary was too great for the slaves to overcome.[1] Nevertheless, despite the slaves' numerous heroic achievements within slavery, real institutional boundaries and obstacles restricted and shaped the African American experience in profound ways. Too often historians overlook or downplay these boundaries for fear of conjuring older images of African Americans as helpless, dehumanized drones. This is an unnecessary precaution because historians have demonstrated repeatedly the individual and collective strength of African American slaves. Therefore, focusing on barriers within slavery does not mean questioning the value of African American achievements but simply provides evidence for just how deplorable the peculiar institution actually was. The statistical evidence presented in chapter 1 makes clear that one of the ways the institution of slavery shaped the African American experience was by limiting the number of slaves converting to Christianity. The visible signs of slavery's restricting influence over slave conversion fit within three general categories: slave access to religious instruction, the nature of the Christian message offered to slaves, and slave religious identity.

Leaders of the two largest Protestant denominations in the antebellum South described vast areas of their region as being religiously destitute. This absence of religious instruction is a principal reason for reevaluating the percentage of Christians within the slave community. Many southerners of all races simply had little exposure to the Gospel.[2] There is no doubt that the institution of slavery exacerbated this situation, since the regional emphasis on staple crop agriculture created a highly mobile and widely dispersed slave-owning population. The ongoing pursuit during the early to mid-nineteenth century of the Old Southwest's more productive cotton lands only increased the difficulties facing antebellum evangelists by greatly enlarging their field of labor. The Southern Baptists pointed to these difficulties during their biennial convention of 1853. Domestic missionaries complained that they faced great burdens on account of "the great extent of country over which our labors extend, . . . the sparseness of population, the want of facilities of communication and [the difficulty of] receiving intelligence, and the inaccessibility of many of these communities which need aid." Six years later the Domestic and Indian Mission Board continued to lament the difficulties of reaching many slaves: "There are many districts of country, rich planting districts, where the white population is too sparse to demand such gospel provisions. Unless special missions are made to these blacks they must live and die without the gospel."[3] Indeed, a quick perusal of a few antebellum descriptions of religious life indicates a variety of obstacles that limited an individual's access to worship. Illness, great distances to meeting places, rain, high water, absent plantation owners, and sea island hopping in small craft are but a few of the obstacles and dangers many southerners faced in seeking to deliver or hear the Gospel. In fact, many of the areas targeted for missions were considered dangerous and claimed the lives of numerous missionaries.[4] How many potential missionaries were deterred by such conditions from entering the mission field cannot be known, but the danger of the work must have been an impediment in recruiting ministers in order to extend the areas served by slave missions.

Where missionaries did make an appearance, many found circumstances similar to those described by an Alabama minister: "The people are generally very poor, and have but little opportunity of going
out of the neighborhood to hear preaching; and those desiring to hear
the word of God are deprived of that blessing for months. There are
many who seldom appear at a place of worship. Not a few spend the
Sabbath in hunting, fishing, shooting at a mark, &c. There are many
families in which there is not a religious person; and many which, until I came here had no Bible, no religious book, and scarcely any kind
of books at all. Children, not a few from 10 to 15 years old there are
who have seldom or never entered a place of worship." Mother Hyacinth LeConnait, a Catholic missionary to northern Louisiana, offered
a similar assessment of her mission field: "These people need much
good example, counsel, to redeem themselves to live in a much more
edifying way. To my knowledge, the American farmer is as far away
from the good Lord as the savage indian is."[5]

Further complicating the issue of southern religious destitution
was the ever-present shortage of missionaries and preachers. Pleas
about the need for more Christian ministers working in the South lit-
ter the antebellum publications of nearly all denominations. For example, the Alabama Baptist Convention noted that only fourteen of
114 state missionary positions were filled for the year 1846. Likewise,
in 1853, the Synod of Tennessee bluntly stated, "We need means to
support the ministers we have, and we are in great want of more."
Keeping in mind that southern denominations sent many ministers
to serve in cities, rural and frontier areas bore the brunt of this shortage of ministers. Since most slaves lived in areas fitting this description, they were among the population least well-served by the clergy,
even when considering the missions established upon their behalf. In
describing the religious conditions of Louisiana, historian Joe Gray
Taylor wrote that "[n]ot enough priests were stationed in Louisiana
to supply the needs of white communicants; neglect of the blacks was
almost inevitable."[6]

The Episcopal Church blamed some of its ministerial limitations in
the South on a "lack of the missionary spirit." Although their analysis
of the shortage mirrors the complaint of many southern denominations, slavery was also a central cause for the lack of ministers and

missionaries in the South. In particular, slavery greatly limited the number of ministers who were available to serve southern religious needs. The mere presence of slavery kept many northern Christians from entering the South as a ministerial field of labor. Philadelphia's *Christian Observer* argued that slavery prevented ministers from going south because it was "unfavorable to religion, and naturally offensive to ministerial laborers from the North." After 1845, the North-South split of Methodists and Baptists over slavery further limited the pool of available ministers by creating region-specific denominations. Another factor complicating the South's minister shortage was the fact that slave owners were not enthusiastic about allowing unknown individuals preach to their slaves. C. C. Jones argued that the emergence of abolition "agitated the public mind within our borders," arrested efforts to convert the slaves in many places, and forced some clergy "to quit the field." This was particularly true after Nat Turner used religious imagery to motivate his Southampton compatriots. Several decades after these bloody events, the Richmond *Christian Advocate* still proclaimed that preaching to slaves "cannot be performed by strangers" and that religious instruction must be "taught by those who have the confidence of the community." In 1836 Methodist minister Joseph Travis was threatened with imprisonment by Mississippi authorities if he dared preach to African Americans and had his services monitored by a "Committee of Vigilance." Likewise, Bishop Augustin Verot of St. Augustine, Florida, noted in 1860 that "many masters do not like for us to preach to these Negroes for fear that they will be given ideas which are now far from their heads." Thus, the fear of further slave uprisings meant that many ministers entering a new region found themselves the subject of suspicion or isolation until they could prove their loyalty with regard to the slavery issue.[7]

The shortage of preachers and rural isolation meant that most southerners had limited and irregular access to religious instruction. In most cases, those with regular access to religious services met only once or twice a month.[8] Slave testimony suggests that religious exercises could be even more infrequent than that. Virginia slave Fleming Clark recalled that "[w]e had no school or church. We were too far away for church." Ann Hawthorne noted "I never hear nuthin' 'bout church 'till way after freedom." Likewise, Josephine Bristow of South Carolina stated that "us didn't go to no church neither cause we was way off dere on de plantation en wasn' any church nowhe' 'bout dere." Both Hattie Sugg of Mississippi and Louisa Adams of North Carolina indicated that they attended church only one time during slavery. Similarly, by age twenty-one, James Pennington of Maryland had heard only two sermons and seen one copy of the New Testament. Finally, Arkansas slave Betty Brown remembered that church services came only once a year in the form of a camp meeting: "We diden' know what church wuz . . . an' the whites nevuh neither. Dey wuz a couple o' men us' ta come by an' hole a camp-meetin'. . . . [D]ey'd come aftuh crops wuz laid by an preach 'til cotton wuz openin'."⁹

Of course, the irregularity of worship services only affected those slaves who were allowed to attend church at all. Not all masters were Christians, and even some who claimed allegiance to Jesus Christ did not allow their slaves to attend worship. Thomas Jones described how his master's rejection of Christianity affected his own faith. Jones declared, "I have at times given up prayer and hope together, believing that my master's words were true, that 'religion is a cursed mockery, and the Bible a lie.'" C. C. Jones acknowledged that all masters were not Christians by dedicating a portion of his book on the religious instruction of slaves to address masters who refused slaves access to Christianity and non-Christian masters who believed they were "excused from the duty." Jones's concerns were validated by the survey conducted for this study which demonstrated that 18.1 percent of all slaves could not attend any form of Christian worship. However, the recollections of unconverted slaves in the survey indicated that masters barred slightly over 30 percent from going to church. Therefore, as the majority of slaves surveyed were unconverted and the survey methodology inflated the number of converted slaves, the percentage of slaves barred from worship was undoubtedly higher than 18.1 percent. This is particularly true given the survey's lenient criteria for identifying a master as allowing worship.¹⁰ More likely, at least one out of four slaves was prohibited from attending any form of Christian services.

Having a master who "allowed" slaves access to worship also did not mean that all slaves on a given farm or plantation could attend church services. Numerous slaves described how some masters permitted

only a select few to attend church with them. Callie Bracey of Mississippi recalled, "On special occasions, the older slaves were allowed to
go to the church of their master." On the Georgia plantation where
Emma Jones lived, only house slaves could join the family in nightly
scripture readings. "[S]laves that could be trusted" went to church
where David Hall lived in North Carolina, while John Becton recalled
that only "coach drivers" were permitted to attend church with their
masters.[11]

John Becton's recollections identify a very special segment of the
slaves who attended worship along with their masters: those that went
in order to serve their owners' needs. Sylvia Cannon had to care for
the masters' baby while she attended their South Carolina brush arbor church. When accompanying her mistress to the Episcopal Church
in Alabama, Sally Murphy "sot in de foot of her carriage" in order to
"open gates and hold de horses." Manda Boggan provided a wide number of services for her masters who attended church. "Us waited on
'em, toted in water an' tended ter de chilluns. When de meetin' wuz
ober us kotched de horses an' led 'em to deir blocks an' brung de car-
riages 'round fer 'em." For many slaves, these Sunday duties gutted the
church services of any special meaning. One slave who had to tend to
the children outside the church while her masters worshiped inside
bitterly recalled that as a result of her duties "I was almost grown before I had ever heard the Bible read and the word of God explained."
Others, however, managed to extract some value out of their unique
form of Sunday "services." The coachman on the plantation where
Silas Jackson lived would listen to the services while waiting to drive
his owners home. As a result of his greater familiarity with the Gospel
message preached in the masters' church, the coachman, Sandy Jas-
par, served as the slaves' preacher.[12]

Even if a master allowed slaves to attend worship with them or hold
their own services, very few did so without imposing restrictions or
special conditions on slave participation. Masters often gave overseers
the discretion to determine who could attend church or required them
to monitor any services where their slaves were present. Overseer discretion was then a common barrier for many slaves who wanted to
attend church. Both Susan Bledsoe of Tennessee and Ella Grandberry
of Alabama noted that slaves could not go to church unless a white

person or overseer went with them. If no whites were willing to go to church, then the slaves could not attend that day. Overseers could also use church attendance to influence slave behavior. The overseer in charge of Mrs. Lou Griffin exemplifies this practice, for he allowed only those slaves who "suited" him to attend Sunday services. Isaac Martin noted that slaves who misbehaved had to work on Sundays and were not allowed to attend church. Where an overseer determined that church services undermined his authority, he could oppose religious instruction in all cases. For instance, Mississippi slave Henry Cheatam accused his overseer of attempting to keep all slaves from going to church or holding any meetings of their own. Huckstep, the overseer in charge of James Williams, went even further in opposing Christianity among the slaves. According to Williams, "Huckstep was himself an open infidel as well as blasphemer. He used to tell the hands that there was no hell hereafter for white people, but that they had their punishment on earth in being obliged to take care of the negroes. As for the blacks, he was sure there was a hell for them. He used frequently to sit with his bottle by his side, and his Bible in his hand, and read passages and comment on them, and pronounce them lies." Given the behavior of some overseers like Huckstep, it is not surprising to find slaves like Joseph Farley and Green Willbanks, who believed it was easier for slaves to obtain passes for visiting, dancing, and playing music than it was for attending religious services.[13]

Masters also shaped the slaves' religious exercises in other ways. Perhaps because of space limitations, work requirements, or fear of large slave gatherings, Spencer Barnett's master made the slaves take turns attending church. Randall Lee's Virginia master allowed his slaves to hold as many prayer meetings as they wished but "did not allow much preaching in the church." Conversely, the master of Millie Simpkins found slave prayer objectionable. "Shouting" slaves had their hands burned where O. W. Green lived, but the master of Siney Bonner only required religious enthusiasts to use an overturned kettle to keep the volume down. Other masters entirely forbid their slaves from participating in any aspect of the church services they attended. According to Anna Scott, "The slaves were forbidden to sing, talk, or make any sound" at church, "under penalty of severe beatings." In addition to receiving beatings, slaves who did not worship in accordance with the masters' desire might lose their religious privileges altogether. For instance, the Baptist Church in Elkton, Kentucky, unanimously adopted the following resolution in 1846: "Resolved that it is the opinion of this church that the meetings of the colored people conducted as they are, are of no benefit to them either in a religious or cival [sic] point of view and that the secston [sic] of this church be instructed not to allow them the use of this house any more for that purpose." The message of the resolution is as clear today as it undoubtedly was for the slave members of the Elkton Baptist Church. While salvation was an individual choice free from external interference, how, when, and where the slaves celebrated that heavenly gift was subject to white approval and control. C. C. Jones pointedly made this clear in declaring that masters "may, according to the power lodged in our hands, forbid religious meetings, and religious instruction on our own plantations; we may forbid our servants going to church at all, or only to such churches as we may select for them; we may literally shut up the kingdom of heaven against men, and suffer not them that are entering to go in!"[14]

While these religious restrictions had the consequence of easing the masters' fear of religion-induced rebellion, the white micromanagement of the slaves' religious life also limited the communal spirit and satisfaction that some slaves drew from Christianity. The words of Mingo White testify to the destructive effect that such precautionary measures had on slave conversion: "Us didn' have nowhar to go 'cep' church an' we didn' git no pleasure outten it 'case we warn't 'lowed to talk from de time we lef' home 'twell we got back." Ella Grandberry echoes White's remarks and demonstrates how masters' religious restrictions affected the slaves' church attendance. "On Sundays us jes' laid 'roun' mos' all day. Us didn't git no pleasure outten goin' to church, 'caze we warn't 'lowed to say nothin'."[15] Such remarks leave little doubt that white efforts to shape the slaves' religious expressions in effect limited both their access to and interest in Christianity.

Of all the obstacles hampering the slaves' access to Christianity, none was greater than the prohibition against teaching bondsmen to read. Clearly, understanding the central tenets of a religion is a vital part of being a believer. Since Christianity's central tenets appear in the Bible as written word, literacy greatly facilitates Christian religious instruction. Interested persons can examine the faith on their

own rather than having to trust the words of someone perhaps unknown to them. Literacy and access to religious literature would also
allow an individual to pursue religious studies in the absence of clergy,
an advantage southern ministers could have utilized in their efforts
to convert the slaves. Southern Baptists readily acknowledged the importance of literacy for slave conversion, declaring, "The reading of his
word we consider next in importance to the preaching of it." So important was literacy for conversion that one of the first acts of the Southern Baptist Convention after the Civil War was to establish and encourage schools among the freedmen. However, in spite of the obvious
religious advantages literacy afforded, most southern states prohibited
teaching slaves to read for fear of triggering insurrection and helping runaways forge passes. In addition, "[b]y 1855 nine of the fifteen
slave states had made it illegal to distribute Bibles among the slaves."[16]

By denying slaves literacy, slave owners in effect required that most
slaves come into contact with persons familiar with the Gospel. While
many African Americans did an admirable job of spreading the Christian message within their own community, in most cases the prohibition of literacy meant that white Christians were the largest source
of religious information available to the slaves. In a region desper-
ately short of regular preaching, the burden of slave conversion fell
largely on the slaveholders themselves. This meant that slaves of non-
Christian masters faced the previously discussed possibility of being
shut off from any religious instruction. Furthermore, as most slave
owners obeyed the state literacy laws pertaining to slaves, Christian
masters typically had to sell the message of salvation to persons who
could not verify the validity of the masters' scriptural interpretation.[17]
Such a situation required a great amount of trust between the com-
municator and his audience. As trust between the races was rare on
most southern farms, Christian slaveholders faced tremendous institutional obstacles in converting their illiterate slaves.

The testimony of many ministers, slave owners, and slaves shows
that catechizing the slaves orally was a less efficient and tedious
means of converting African Americans. Concerned Christians particularly complained that by stripping literacy training from religious
education, southern lawmakers removed a key incentive for slave attendance of church services and made instruction more difficult.

For example, the Moravian missionaries to slaves in North Carolina blamed a considerable decline in African American attendance of Sunday schools on the fact that they were "no longer permitted to teach them to read." Plantation mistresses, on whom the task of catechizing slaves usually fell, expressed similar frustrations about the difficulties of teaching an illiterate people the word of God. In 1860, Catherine Edmondston recorded in her diary her feelings about the effectiveness of catechisms for teaching slaves about Christianity and attracting them to the faith:

> I heard all that Gatty calls the "sponsible ones" say their cat-echism, but I do not hope for much from it. It is uphill work and ought to be done more regularly than I do it. Bishop Ives cat-echism I do not like at all; the repetition is tiresome. . . . They learn nothing from me but the mere rudiments of Christianity —who made them, who Redeemed them, with the certainty of a future of reward or punishment, the Creed, the ten Command-ments, & exhortations against lying & stealing—and only the little ones get that. They will not come to church even when Pat-rick has it for them.

Mary Boykin Chesnut expressed great admiration for a minister's success in teaching the catechism to slaves because her own efforts had fallen woefully short. Chesnut admitted to her diary in 1861 that after failing to teach her slaves the catechism she "let my Sunday School all drift into singing hymns." Rather than continue her effort to provide religious instruction other than hymns, she decided it would be better "to wait until they developed more brains."[18]

The religious ignorance that Chesnut saw as resulting from a lack of brains was more properly understood by the slaves to be due to a lack of literacy and proper instruction. Minksie Walker complained of such in her description of the worship services she attended as a slave in Tennessee: "De meeting was about like it is now 'cept we didn't know half de time what dey was talking about, we couldn't read and learn."[19] Further complicating this fact was the racist assumption that ministers had to tailor religious instruction "to the capacity of their minds."[20] This meant that much of the religious education provided to slaves was overly simplistic. In fact, many of the catechisms used to instruct the slaves doubled as children's religious literature.[21] South Carolina slave Ervin Smith remembered his basic catechism lessons of "Who made you?" and "Why ought you to love God?" well into the twentieth century. However, while Smith easily remembered his catechism lessons, he blamed its brief questionnaire form for providing slaves with too little knowledge about Christianity.[22] Perhaps it was for this reason that Arie Binns described white preaching as being no more than "long tiresome sermons."[23] Indeed, anyone who has sat through an exhortation on the doctrinal differences between various denominations can imagine the frustration that an illiterate slave might feel while taking in a Sunday sermon on transubstantiation or predestination. That many ministers did preach about subjects that were beyond the slaves' knowledge base is clear. As late as 1861, Charles Colcock Jones, an experienced and concerned missionary to the slaves, continued to admonish many of his fellow ministers for preaching above the understanding of their congregations. Jones openly lamented that despite decades of advice from missionaries involved among the slaves, "[m]uch of our preaching does not reach our congregations."[24]

Ironically, most African Americans found the messages that did reach their congregations lacking in value. To begin with, the Christian New Testament suggests that only a small percentage of people hearing the message of Jesus Christ will respond to the Nazarene's teachings. In the Gospel of Matthew, Jesus commands his followers to symbolically "[e]nter through the narrow gate. For wide is the gate and broad is the road that leads to destruction, and many enter through it. But small is the gate and narrow the road that leads to life, and only a few find it."[25] In other words, many people simply do not find the message of Christianity appealing no matter how clearly or enthusiastically it is preached. C. C. Jones put it succinctly in writing, "All men have not faith."[26] However, if Christian theology suggests that only a few follow the path to salvation under normal circumstances, African Americans living under the institution of slavery often found the path blocked by man-made obstacles.

Numerous slaves testified that the Christian message presented to them during slavery was of little appeal for them. The two principal causes for this lack of appeal were the content of the sermons preached to slaves and the hypocritical actions of many southern

Christians. These two factors together created such negative feelings about southern Christianity that it is not hard to imagine that a majority of the slaves might have rejected the faith offered them.

African American slaves lived in an extremely restrictive environment. While it was not the totally closed system that Elkins described, the institution of slavery did limit free expression, movement, familial and personal relationships, as well as control over the slaves' bodies.[27] Because whites dictated so much of their lives, slaves rejoiced in the liberties they were allowed, bargained for, or took covertly. As Levine and Abrahams demonstrate, music and dance were two of the principal areas of African American independence and creativity.[28] Frolics and corn shuckings provided slaves with important opportunities for allowing individual expression and strengthening communal ties. However, the evangelical Christianity of the slaves prohibited dancing and secular music, thus reducing the slaves' already limited social space even further. In addition to these restrictions, Christianity teaches that lying, stealing, and physical resistance to worldly authorities are also inappropriate behavior. Trapped in an environment where honesty and obedience could mean hunger, exile, physical abuse, and death, slaves understandably found that such injunctions only complicated an already difficult situation. Faced with such a scenario, it would not be surprising if most slaves found these conditions reason enough for not converting to Christianity. This is not to suggest that slaves were libertines devoid of morality. Slaves of many religious backgrounds struggled admirably to forge their own moral order within an immoral institution. But the slaves were human, and adding new restrictions to an already fettered world could only prove irksome. This is especially true since the heavenly master's words usually came out of the mouths of men demanding earthly obedience to themselves.

Indeed, the slaves' most consistent complaint against the teachings of the various Christian denominations was the nearly omnipresent focus on the theme of "[s]ervants, be obedient to your masters."[29] Plagued by nightmarish visions of slaves using biblical inspiration to rise and destroy the South's peculiar institution, southern slaveholders typically demanded that Christians present African Americans with a limited version of their Gospel message. For example, in response to the abolitionist threat, Methodist missionary William Capers promised South Carolinians "[o]ur missionaries inculcate the duties of servants to their masters, as we find those duties stated in the scriptures." Rather than lose access to the slaves or threaten the social structure they embraced, southern Christians like Capers willingly constructed a slave-specific version of the Gospel that emphasized otherworldly salvation in exchange for moral behavior and earthly obedience to whites. In fact, southern Christians routinely gained access to the slaves by touting the Gospel's potential for producing good order on a plantation as a selling point.[30]

Both Genovese and Raboteau argue that this eclectic form of the Christian Gospel provided slave and master benefits since it identified duties that each party owed to the other. In contrast, Margaret Creel argues that most religious messages did not emphasize such reciprocity. Specifically, her research on Gullah religion identified an abundance of literature articulating the duties of slaves to masters but very little discussing the duties of masters to slaves. The research presented here suggests that Creel's view is the more accurate of the two arguments. Most slaves complained that discussions of Christian duties focused solely on their obligations to the master. Furthermore, while Genovese argues that the slaves saw through the masters' religious duplicity and extracted their own value from Christianity, the findings of this study suggest that many slaves extracted little from the faith offered them and as a result many of them rejected it.[31]

Charles Ball made an acute observation in explaining why his African grandfather rejected Christianity. As suggested by Genovese, Ball's grandfather did see through the version of Christianity that Maryland slaveholders offered to the slaves. But rather than finding the rudiments of a faith that he could shape and call his own, Ball's grandfather only found "the religion of his oppressors to be the invention of designing men." As a result of his discovery, the old African rejected Christianity and "retained his native traditions." Stories like this would recur repeatedly throughout the antebellum South. In fact, Virginia slave and Baptist minister Peter Randolph argued that the Gospel offered to the slaves "had better be buried in oblivion, for it makes more heathens than Christians." Henry Bibb agreed with Randolph and declared, "This kind of preaching has driven thousands into

infidelity." Emma Tidwell elaborated on such criticism by characterizing sermons to the slaves as nothing more than "[m]ind yo mistress.
Don't steal der potatoes; don't lie bout nothin' an don' talk back tuh
yo boss; ifn yo does yo'll be tied tuh a tree an stripped necked. When
dey tell yuh tuh do somethin' run an do hit." Alice Sewell, like many
other slaves, never heard about Jesus or "'bout a slave dying and going
to heaven." Because of such content, Hannah Austin argued that she
and her fellow Georgia slaves "seldom heard a true religious sermon."
Accordingly, such preaching led to much feigned religion and few conversions. Henry Wright argued as much when he noted, "None of the
slaves believed in the sermons but they pretended to do so." Similarly,
Tom Hawkins responded to questions about slave Christianity by asking "How could anybody be converted on dat kind of preachin'[?]"[32]

Given the slaves' reaction to most sermons, the axiom "actions
speak louder than words" had significant meaning for African Americans belonging to or living among professed Christians. Slaves frequently took note of white behavior in view of the spirit of Christianity and made value judgments about the faith based on white efforts
to live up to the ideals of Jesus Christ. Clearly, the inhumane or inconsistent behavior of many professed Christians hindered the effort
to convert the slaves. For example, Cureton Milling's master shocked
him by selling his own mulatto children despite being a member of
the Presbyterian Church. John Smith noted that his master, an un-
married preacher, had several children by his married slave mistress.
Mattie Curtis found fault with her master, also a minister, because he
beat his slaves badly and gave them minimal food. Finally, Leah Garrett criticized the preacher who owned her for whipping an old cook to
death before he left to conduct services one Sunday. The narrative of
Frederick Douglass provides an extremely eloquent and detailed sum-
mation of the disgust that many slaves felt toward southern Christianity because of such failings: "I am filled with unutterable loathing
when I contemplate the religious pomp and show, together with the
horrible inconsistencies, which every where surround me. We have
men-stealers for ministers, women-whippers for missionaries, and
cradle-plunderers for church members. The man who wields the blood-
clotted cowskin during the week fills the pulpit on Sunday, and claims
to be a minister of the meek and lowly Jesus."[33]

Many other narratives demonstrate that African American slaves often doubted or rejected Christianity because the white people around them failed to lead a consistent Christian life. Moses Roper identified his master as "a member of a Baptist church" but pointed out that "[h]is slaves, thinking him a very bad sample of what a professing Christian ought to be, would not join the connexion he belonged to, thinking they must be a very bad set of people." Austin Steward had similar feelings regarding his seemingly pious master. Upon reflecting on how his master severely beat his sister one Sunday morning, Steward proclaimed, "Can any one wonder that I, and other slaves, often doubted the sincerity of every white man's religion? Can it be a matter of astonishment, that slaves often feel that there is no just God for the poor African?" Harriet Jacobs also refused to join the church because her married Episcopalian master continually hounded her for sexual favors. Charles Ball rejected Christianity because after his sale farther south, "I could not pray, for the measure of my woes seemed to be full, and I felt as if there was no mercy in heaven, nor compassion on earth, for a man who was born a slave." Lorendo Goodwin abandoned his Catholic faith after a priest violated the confessional by reporting that his cousin requested prayers in behalf of emancipation. Finally, after his Methodist class leader attempted to kill him, Isaac Mason pondered the validity of Christianity by asking "How could I judge of his religious profession? How could I receive his religious instructions?"[34] Isaac Mason was not alone in his questioning of southern Christian sincerity. Widespread African American doubts about the message and messengers of the church created a spiritual rift between white and black that few were willing to reach across.

American slavery and its emphasis on racial differences created separate identities for white and black members of southern society. The presence of these separate identities complicated and undermined the Christian ideal of unity within the body of Christ. White and black southerners saw each other as being so different that many African Americans simply could not accept the idea of sharing the same beliefs with whites. As with Charles Ball's African grandfather, the religion of their oppressors was not to be believed. While there is evidence that some white and black Christians did enjoy a shared religious experience, most African Americans did not view themselves as a part of white Christianity. Most slaves saw the Gospel offered them as a perversion of the truth or as proof that Christianity was a false religion.[35] In either case, African Americans generally placed little faith in what white Christians had to say about religion. Understandably, such a division hindered the conversion of slaves to Christianity and ultimately contributed to the development of segregated churches.

African American slaves clearly articulated their separate religious identities throughout the narratives, interviews, and autobiographies they have given us. Although many slaves attended integrated services, most did not feel that they were truly a part of those churches. For instance, Mingo White and C. B. Burton described their church attendance in the following manners: According to White, "Us didn't have no church 'cep de white folks church." Similarly, Burton recalled, "We had no school and no church: but was made to go to de white folks church and set in de gallery." In addition to being typical, White and Burton's descriptions both show that they did not invest their spiritual being in the "white folks church." As with most African Americans, that institution was not theirs; it belonged only to the whites. In fact, former slave Georgia Baker even felt great dissatisfaction with the integrated church she joined after the Civil War while living up north. Baker identified her main objection to the church in saying, "Northern churches ain't lak our southern churches 'cause de black and white folkses all belong to de same church. . . . On dat account I still didn't feel lak I had jined de church."[36] To a significant degree, reactions like Baker's stemmed from the belief that racists, especially slaveholders, could not be Christians. Therefore, joining a church that was full of heathens was the spiritual equivalent of not joining a church at all.

Slaves regularly expressed their doubts about the legitimacy of white Christianity. For instance, Lydia Adams was hardly alone when she said, "I don't think any slaveholder can get to the kingdom." Henry Bibb noted that fugitive slaves that had been baptized by slaveholding ministers often had the ritual redone in the North. Others argued that having a Christian master was as bad if not in fact worse than having a nonbelieving owner. Maryland slave Joseph Smith bluntly stated that "I'd rather live with a card-player and a drunkard than with a Christian." Clearly, most slaves did not believe that white and blacks could share the same religious experience. Matilda Perry argued as much when she stated, "White folks can't pray right to the black man's God." Katie Sutton elaborated further about this spiritual separation, "White folks jes' naturally different from darkies. . . . We's different in color, in talk and in 'ligion and beliefs. We's different in every way and can never be spected to think to live alike." American Missionary Association (AMA) teachers working with the freedmen found that this perception of white and black difference hindered some of their efforts to convert African Americans to Christianity. For example, in the Chesapeake region, AMA teachers had some difficulty in getting the older generation of freedmen to read the Bible. According to the teachers, the freedmen hesitated to read scripture because "their masters and families were Bible Christians, and they did not want to be like them."[37]

Many slaves saw whites as not only different but oppositional in nature. As exemplified by their approach to religion, whites and blacks held diametrically opposed beliefs and thus viewed the world with greatly different eyes. For example, while whites believed they preached sound doctrine, slaves believed the messages usually amounted to "all lies" and telling "stories 'bout 'ligion."[38] When southern preachers prayed for Confederate success, slaves like Minnie Davis's mother asked God for northern victory and freedom. Some slaves even believed that contact with whites destroyed African Americans' innate goodness. In Mary Ferguson's eyes, "[C]olored people are naturally religious . . . [but] they learned all their 'devilment' from the whites." Solbert Butler even noted that the freedmen built their churches to face east "[b]ut the white folks church was face west."[39] Thus, in the eyes of many slaves, white and black southerners were spiritually incompatible and did not benefit from the time they spent together in worship.

Because many if not most slaves drew little comfort from the religious aspects of attending church, African Americans routinely used Sundays to meet their own earthly needs. Many African Americans not required to attend church spent Sundays resting from the past week's labor. For example, Wash Hayes of Mississippi recalled, "De slaves mos' an' generally wuz tired out an lay 'round an' rested." Allen Parker offers one explanation for slaves resting on Sunday. In describing frolics Parker noted, "If the next day was Sunday or was a holiday, the dance would continue all night. The young men would dance all

night till broad daylight, and then go home with the girls in the morning." Others used the freedom from work to spend time with their
families and friends on and, if allowed, off of the farm where they
lived. In fact, slaves commonly referred to Sundays as "visitin' day."
M. E. Abrams fondly remembered stealing hogs and enjoying barbecue
and frivolity on Sundays. "As none o' our gang didn't have no 'ligion,
us never felt no scruples bout . . . getting de 'cue' ready fo Sunday."
If her master asked them where they had been that day Abrams admitted, "Us would tell some lie bout gwine to a church 'siety meetin.'"
Other energetic slaves might go to town or the woods to play, court,
gamble, fight, drink, or go dancing. Still more spent the day in productive family labor such as washing clothes or supplementing their
diet with fresh fish. Again, C. C. Jones provides a detailed summary of
the slaves' typical approach to the Sabbath. Jones lamented that "they
spend the day in visiting, in idleness and sleep, or in hunting, fishing,
or sometimes, in thieving or working for their own convenience and
profit; and where Sunday markets are tolerated, in trading." Perhaps it
was these alternatives to church that allowed Frederick Law Olmsted
to observe that of slaves in the vicinity of Richmond "not more than
one-fifth of the negroes living within a convenient distance were in
the habit of attending."[40]

Unconverted slaves who had to attend worship services also used
these events for their own purposes. Slaves often saw worship services
as a relaxing break from the routine of work. Olmsted reported that of
the few slaves who attended worship near Richmond "many came late,
and many more slept through the greater part of the service." According to Hannah Davidson of Kentucky, this was not surprising because
Sunday services were "the only chance we'd get to rest." However, as
Sena Moore discovered when her master whipped her for snoring in
church, slaves had to be very careful not to become too comfortable
during worship services. Nonetheless, Matthew Hume eagerly went
to Catholic catechism class, not for sweet dreams, but for the candy
or sugar his mistress gave to those attending. Likewise, William Wells
Brown enjoyed the sweet taste of secretly imbibed mint juleps during compulsory family prayer meetings. In contrast to Brown, Arthur
Colson and George Morrison used chicanery to pursue more innocent
pastimes. Colson used the distraction of church services to slip outside

and go fishing, while Morrison employed the same scheme to enjoy a game of marbles. Finally, slaves who had no choice but to sit outside of the church during services could use the occasion to entertain themselves at the minister's expense. Horace Tonsler of Virginia described how slaves "would git up outside an' start in to preachin' right along wid preacher Woodson. Softlike, of course, wid a lot of handwavin' an' twistin' of his mouth widdout makin' no noise. We would sit up an' listen to him an laugh when he say just what de preacher say."[41]

As Tonsler's recollection suggests, most African Americans saw church attendance as an opportunity to enjoy the companionship of their fellow slaves. As recalled by North Carolina slave Robert Falls, church was the only place that many slaves were allowed to go to away from their owner's property. Such travel restrictions meant that church provided one of the only sanctioned occasions where large numbers of slaves could meet together in relative peace. As church meetings usually occurred only once or twice a month and often required long-distance travel, Sunday services could last all day and include a scrumptious dinner on the grounds. Likewise, annual camp meetings lasted a week or more and featured large quantities of food. Isaac Stier, like many slaves, remembered the food more than the worship at these events: "Dey cooked up whole trunks full o' good things an' driv' over to de camp grounds. . . . Whilst dey was worshipin' I'd slip 'roun' and tas' out of dey basket. Ever'day I'd eat till I was ready to bus'." Likewise, Tom Mills proclaimed, "They would preach and shout and have a good time and have plenty to eat. That was what most of 'em went for." More importantly, these occasions provided slaves opportunities to renew or begin kinship and friendship ties. Families, separated by sale or interplantation marriage, could reunite at these times and lonely souls could seek out new associations or support networks. Since there were few opportunities for off-property romantic encounters, numerous slaves remembered church services as the time when "boys shined up to de gals." Elisha Garey fondly remembered how "boys and gals done some tall courtin' at dem brush arbors. Dat was de onliest place whar you could get to see de gals you lakked de best." Candis Goodwin recalled how she first met her husband Jake in church: "We all was to church one Sunday, an' Jake he kep' cidin' up to me. An' I's lookin' at him outer de coner o' my eye, till finally he come

up an' took holt o' my hands."[42] Indeed, dressed in their finest clothing, young African American men and women like Candis and Jake
eagerly sought to find potential spouses and lovers from among church
and camp-meeting congregations.

In addition to food and fellowship, camp meetings, unlike church
services, provided slaves with a brief but significant amount of freedom. While whites closely monitored the behavior of slaves sitting
in a church balcony, camp meetings took on an almost circuslike at-
mosphere where one could more easily slip away unnoticed by the
master's watchful eye. Minister and former Tennessee slave J. W.
Loguen provided an eloquent description of the carnivalesque quali-
ties of an antebellum camp meeting in his mid-nineteenth-century
autobiography.

> As a general thing, the slaves also were there, as servants of
> their masters and mistresses, or to enjoy a holiday of personal
> relaxation and pleasure, or to sell the fruits some of them were
> allowed to raise on their little patches of ground. The free blacks
> and poor whites were there also, with meats, fruits, and liquors
> of various kinds, to sell to the white aristocrats, who from pride,
> or fashion, or religion, were attracted to the place. The camp was
> the universal resort of lovers and rowdies, politicians and plea-
> sure seekers of every kind, as well as religionists, who gathered
> about the preachers, or promenaded in the woods, or refreshed
> at the booths, where the poor whites and blacks exposed their
> provisions for sale.[43]

Obviously, camp meetings offered something for everyone, and the
slaves relished the memories of the temporary freedom provided by
these annual events. For example, John Hill remembered that during
the slaves' annual August camp meeting the whites "fixed good din-
ners for us, an' let us go off in de woods an' stay all day." Despite not
caring much about church, William Byrd described camp meetings
as being great "cause you could see every body two or three counties
around. . . . [and] They let's the negro do most as he pleased there sos
he behaved his self."[44]

As the preceding evidence suggests, many slaves routinely attended church services for a multitude of reasons other than seeking

conversion. Again, this evidence underscores the need for scholars to separate antebellum African American church attendance from actual conversion to Christianity. Furthermore, when viewed alongside the barriers hindering slave conversion, this evidence also suggests that slavery was far from a Christianizing institution. In fact, as presented here, slavery was a major hindrance for Christians concerned about the souls of slaves. While slavery brought Africans and African Americans into proximity with Christianity, the institution as established in the United States made conversions difficult and, in some cases, virtually impossible.

In summary, slavery helped create regional settlement patterns that made regular contact with religious instruction the exception rather than the rule for most slaves. Furthermore, the religious and ideological debates surrounding slavery only exacerbated this situation by limiting the already small number of ministers available to preach in the South. African American access to religious instruction depended upon the attitude and actions of the slave owners. As shown, non-Christian masters or those with only a slight interest in religion were often less than enthusiastic about or openly hostile to the idea of evangelizing their slaves. Such apathy or hostility meant that many slaves could not attend Christian services even if they were available. Finally, institutional safeguards like the prohibition of literacy, the monitoring of services, and a limited Gospel message made the transmission of religious ideas more difficult and less compelling. Countless slaves found the message offered to them grounded in hypocrisy or unappealing. As a result, it is not unreasonable to suggest that most slaves simply did not become Christians.

Nineteenth-century Christians recognized that slavery as it existed in the United States prevented many slaves from converting. In particular, Christians realized that allowing imperfect humans to own their fellow man placed too many African Americans in a condition of spiritual neglect. In order to call attention to this problem, Christians from many denominations openly criticized their own lack of effort to evangelize the slaves and repeatedly called on masters to live up to their moral duties to their bondsmen. For example, William Wightman, Methodist minister and biographer of William Capers, wrote that despite Reverend Capers's heroic efforts "it is not claimed that any very extraordinary success in the conversion of the blacks has crowned the exertions of the missionaries." Methodists blamed their less-than-extraordinary results on the fact that as of 1858 "we have as yet very imperfectly entered into the work which God has assigned us." Episcopalians described their efforts as "ineffective" and noted that "[i]t has been painfully experienced, heretofore, in the acknowledged fact that our missionary contributions have not been made according to the high standard of the Gospel." As late as 1863, the Ten Islands Baptist Association of Alabama complained that "while some churches and some masters seem alive to the subject, too many seem to neglect to a great extent the religious instruction of this class of our population." Even C. C. Jones believed that African Americans exhibited a poor moral and religious condition because of "the little, comparatively speaking, that we are doing for them." According to Jones, this inattention created the circumstance where "[t]he number of professors of religion, in proportion to the whole, is not large."[45]

Such self-flagellation in part reflects the deep concern that many committed Christians had about the spiritual state of the slaves. However, it also reflects the fact that heartfelt ideals espoused on a national level did not always affect local circumstances. For example, despite decades of regionwide preaching about the need to increase the slaves' religious privileges, C. C. Jones's highly praised efforts in Liberty County, Georgia, did not even produce similar results throughout his home state. Specifically, in 1860, Liberty County had enough church pews to accommodate over 146 percent of its population. In contrast, a survey of the other nine leading black-majority counties in Georgia shows that they averaged enough church pews to seat only 48.8 percent of their residents.[46] Obviously, while many pointed to Liberty County as worthy of emulation, few followed their pioneering example. Likewise, the decentralized organizational structure of the Southern Baptists meant that local religious bodies did not have to implement policies recommended by the denominational convention. As late as 1859, the Southern Baptist Convention had to stir their churches into action on behalf of the slaves by pleading, "Shall we not—ought we not to feel a deeper interest in this work?"[47] Such pleas reveal the frustration that many missionary agencies felt about the recurrent reports of ministerial destitution that hindered missions to the slaves. For example, in 1857, the Bethel Baptist Association of Alabama awaited "the time . . . when the colored man's spiritual interest will be regarded according to its magnitude, and corresponding efforts be put forth for its promotion."[48] Six years later, Alabama Baptists still waited for their season of awakening as they openly acknowledged that the slaves' "moral and spiritual culture have been sadly neglected."[49] However, Alabamians were not alone in admitting their neglect of African American spiritual needs. In the wake of Confederate defeat, Christians throughout the South openly acknowledged that they had not lived up to their moral obligations to the slaves and interpreted the Civil War and emancipation as God's punishment for their negligence.[50]

3

ALTERNATIVES TO CHRISTIANITY WITHIN
THE ANTEBELLUM SLAVE COMMUNITY

I assisted her and her husband to inter the infant—which was a little boy—and its father buried with it a small bow and several arrows; a little bag of parched meal; a miniature canoe, about a foot long, and a little paddle, (with which he said it would cross the ocean to his own country) a small stick, with an iron nail, sharpened, and fastened into one end of it; and a piece of white muslin, with several curious and strange figures painted on it in blue and red, by which he said, his relations and countrymen would know the infant to be his son, and would receive it accordingly, on its arrival amongst them.
—CHARLES BALL, *Fifty Years in Chains*

He thinks there are spirits that direct your life and if you do wrong the evil fates let you be punished. He believes in good and evil spirits. Spirits right here among us.
—NARRATIVE OF GEORGE BRADDOX, in Rawick, *American Slave*

Acc: ccording to John S. Mbiti, Africans are deeply religious people. In Africa "[r]eligion permeates into all the departments of life so fully that it is not easy or possible always to isolate it." In other words, for Africans of many different backgrounds, life and religion merge so completely that everyday activities and acts of worship are often one and the same. To live is to believe in and interact with things spiritual or supernatural.[1] Those Africans who came to North America as slaves were no different. Their forced migration across the Atlantic introduced a wide variety of religious beliefs into the American landscape. Despite slaveholders' opposition to African religious practices and the mid-nineteenth-century effort to convert them to Christianity, Africans and African Americans continued to pursue their ancestral religious beliefs well into the nineteenth century.[2] While no single African religious system survived unchanged, it is not unreasonable to argue that many if not most believers continued to practice their faiths to the best of their abilities. These faiths would have varied but would likely have featured elements of ancestor veneration, polytheism, and an active linkage between the living and the dead as well as a merging of the natural and supernatural realms. These various forms of African religious practice, particularly the spiritually informed practice of conjure, may have served to organize the slaves' worldview in many ways far more than did Christianity.

In contrast to the preceding statement, most contemporary historians argue that the introduction of diverse African peoples among the plantations and farms of America disrupted much if not most of the enslaved persons' cultures. The argument goes that Africans, unable to speak one another's languages or being of rival cultures and living together on disparate, isolated farms, could neither fully maintain nor successfully pass on their traditional cultures to future generations. Therefore, with each passing generation, more and more of the slaves' African heritage disappeared or became incomprehensible to their American-born children. Whites, seeing African cultures as uncivilized or the breeding ground for rebellion, accelerated this process of cultural disintegration by prohibiting most public displays of the slaves' ancestral customs. Eventually, the elements of the slaves' African heritage that managed to survive this process merged into a unified African American culture via their common use of the English language, interregional migration, and similar life experiences in North America. Of course, as previously described, this interpretation places Afro-Christianity squarely in the center of the resulting African American culture.[3]

What is curious about this interpretation is its assertion that the slaves could recall the inclusion within their traditional religion of elements such as a single creator God, symbolic death and rebirth, water as a spiritual symbol, blood sacrifice, religious prayer and song, and an afterlife, yet they could not maintain or devise a coherent belief system. Instead, so the story goes, most African Americans converted to a modified form of Christianity that emphasized the similarities between their new and ancestral faiths. This scenario is puzzling to say the least. As Anthony B. Pinn points out, prior to the Great Awakenings of the eighteenth and nineteenth centuries there was more than a hundred-year period "during which complex African traditions could have taken root." Given the acknowledged similarities between different West African religious traditions, it is quite likely that the slaves did find enough common ground to forge African composite religions rather than merely adapting African beliefs to Christianity. Furthermore, the notion that the ancient and largely oral cultures of Africa could not pass on some of their religious ideas to their children is questionable. Protestant peasants survived the struggles of the Reformation in Europe with their faith intact. Jewish beliefs and communities outlasted centuries of pogroms and religious persecution. Catholic and Mormon religious beliefs survived mob violence and government-sanctioned prohibitions in the United States. Why should African beliefs have been less apt to survive, especially since widespread efforts to convert the slaves did not begin in earnest until the 1830s? Philip D. Morgan argues that "[t]he vast majority of eighteenth-century Anglo-American slaves lived and died strangers to Christianity." For the current interpretation of Afro-Christianity to hold true, the American slave community would have had to undergo a massive conversion and also reach communal spiritual maturity between 1830 and 1865. This is a highly unlikely scenario. Additionally, scholars already acknowledge that secret Afro-Christian worship services occurred despite white opposition. To suggest that other religious groups could not succeed in similar fashion is to disregard the very arguments scholars use to demonstrate African American agency during slavery. Some scholars recognize this inconsistency and have suggested that secret non-Christian worship services were a part of the slaves' religious activities. Virginia slave Isaac Williams suggested as much in recalling, "I heard of some that believed in voodouism and fetishism, but never saw any of their religious rites performed, though I believe that further south they practiced many superstitious observances."[4]

In fairness to most modern scholars and earlier observers of slave religion, there is much about the African American religious experience that defies quick recognition or discovery. As stated earlier, slave religion was in many cases a covert practice. Given the slaves' covert religious activities and white opposition to these practices, it is understandable that descriptions of such worship services are scarce. Where informants have provided descriptions of religious practices, it is likely that most African Americans did not reveal practices that would be considered non-Christian. Indeed, late nineteenth- and early twentieth-century African American elites sought to pull their freedmen brethren closer to societal norms so as to gain acceptance within a racist, white-dominated nation. In order to accomplish this, the retention of African customs and beliefs was opposed, denied, or recast into a Christian mold. For example, the postbellum emphasis on the preservation of slave spirituals overshadowed the equally significant tradition of non-Christian music among the slaves. Austin Grant is not unusual in regard to the decline of that musical tradition. Grant remembered, "On Saturday night they . . . would jes sing at their own houses. Oh, yes'm I 'member 'em singin' 'Run, nigger, Run' but it's too far back for me to 'member those other songs. They would raise up a song when they was pickin' cotton, but I don' 'member much about those songs." According to historian Dena J. Epstein, this eclipsing of the slaves' other music reflects a conscious effort by missionaries to suppress traditions that were "unworthy of rising free men." The findings of this study also suggest that newly converted freedmen rejected secular music traditions in favor of what they found to be more edifying forms. Such efforts allowed African Americans to appear more American than African and helped vindicate the cost of the Civil War by portraying it as a moral contest fought by and for a Christian people.[5] Clearly, as slaves and freedmen understood the need to conform at least publicly to white societal norms, the scarcity of sources on non-Christian religious practices is not surprising.

Of equal importance to the scarcity of sources for non-Christian religious behavior within the slave community is the white observers' unfamiliarity with and inability to detect such beliefs. First of all, as demonstrated in earlier chapters, many southern Christians lamented that most masters took little interest in the spiritual lives of their slaves. Apparently, as long as there were no disruptions on the farm most masters did not care what their slaves believed. This general willful ignorance permitted many things to go undetected. For example, overconfidence or self-delusion allowed the slaves to shock slave owners by flocking to Union lines and freedom during the Civil War. Many slave owners had assumed that they knew and could control what lay within their slaves' hearts but found that they had been wrong. Archaeology shows that masters were no more successful in controlling the physical behavior of their slaves: excavations frequently reveal evidence of theft, plantation sabotage, gun ownership, and even literacy among the slaves. Simply put, if masters could not completely control the physical behavior of African American slaves, they had even less control over their religious beliefs. Margaret Washington Creel argues as much in her interpretation of Gullah religion by saying that slaves rejected orthodox Christianity but duped masters into believing that they had embraced the faith by participating in approved religious activities. Such deception should not be a surprise for scholars who routinely describe the slaves' love for "'puttin' Ole Massa on." Missionaries like C. C. Jones were certainly not surprised by such behavior. In describing the challenges of bringing slaves into the church, Jones complained, "They are one thing before the whites, and another before their own color."[6] One can hardly imagine a greater sense of accomplishment than fooling the master into believing that his control-centered religion had you under control.

Not only is it unlikely that most slaves would have openly revealed non-Christian religious beliefs; it is also highly improbable that white southerners would have acknowledged the existence of such beliefs. By admitting the presence of non-Christian religious beliefs among the slaves, masters would have undermined their argument for slavery as a Christianizing institution. Unquestionably, mid-nineteenth-century masters were not going to provide abolitionists with such solid evidence to use against the peculiar institution. After the Civil War, the African American elites' effort to wipe away African elements of their culture meshed quite well with the desires of white southerners. For white southerners, the denial of late nineteenth-century African religious traditions validated their belief in slavery as a divine institution that uplifted the savage to salvation. It also reinforced racist notions of the superiority of white over black culture and provided another argument for minimizing African American contributions to American society. Folklorist Guy B. Johnson sums up this racist line of thinking by arguing that it is the "overwhelming tendency of the culture of the white man to displace the Negro's African culture, and that their influence . . . is relatively inconsequential."[7] Thus, neither before nor immediately after the Civil War, was it in the interest of whites to disclose evidence of the presence of African religions in the antebellum South.

Another factor to consider is that most white southerners would not have recognized the subtle signs of an African religion. More specifically, if a person was unaware of the meaning of a religious item, he would be less likely to interpret that item as being tied to religion. For instance, if one is unfamiliar with Christianity, he is not going to understand the importance of wearing symbols such as a crucifix. Thus, while masters knew their slaves had African origins, most paid little attention to the nuances of West African religions. Therefore, it is quite likely that countless masters misinterpreted or ignored outward signs of non-Christian religious behavior as mere expressions of an African aesthetic or superstition. This is especially true since most of the materials used by slaves for religious rituals were reworked items of European-American origin. In this way, African beliefs became camouflaged by Euro-American appearances.[8] However, as demonstrated by a nineteenth-century Muslim prayer from Brazil, such potential misinterpretations are not limited to the realm of personal adornment.

(1) in the name of the compassionate merciful God. praise
(2) God master of the worlds, the compassionate the merciful
(3) Lord of judgment day. we love thee
(4) and from thee we ask for help. lead us in the path
(5) of righteousness, in the path of those thou
(6) didst favor and who are not the object of thy
(7) wrath and not the wayward amen[9]

Clearly, it would take a keen ear and a familiarity with Islam to identify an English translation of this prayer as not being an offering to the Christian God. That North American masters were unlikely to make such an identification and therefore prohibit this practice needs no further explanation.

Despite the limitations for identifying African religions within the antebellum slave population, ample evidence suggests that such faiths did exist among the bondsmen. The works of Allan D. Austin, Michael A. Gomez, and Sylviane A. Diouf all demonstrate that Islam survived beyond emancipation among a small but devoted segment of the United States' slave population.[10] Each author uses the standard documentary sources of slavery, the WPA narratives and autobiographies, to demonstrate that Islam has been a much-neglected aspect in the historiography of slave religion. To correct this oversight, Austin collected and published a significant body of primary data and historical accounts about Muslim slaves in the United States and North America. Significantly, this collection contains data that provide substance to the interpretation of this study. For instance, as previously argued, slaves often duped their masters into believing that they had accepted Christianity while pursuing traditional beliefs instead.

Austin recalls the life story of Abdul Rahahman, a Muslim slave in antebellum Mississippi whose pretense of practicing Christianity was extraordinarily elaborate. Abdul Rahahman was so trusted by his master that he was given the job of managing the plantation on which he lived. After serving his master for forty years, Rahahman secured his freedom and planned to return to Africa. Impressed by Rahahman's intelligence, literacy, and manner, members of the American Colonization Society sent him on a fund- and consciousness-raising tour of the nation. The society promised Rahahman that the tour would allow him to raise funds not only for the organization but also for purchasing the freedom of his wife and children in Mississippi. Rahahman was a convincing advocate for the organization and assured supporters that he would use his influence in Africa to spread the Christian gospel and secure new ties for American businesses in his homeland. The tour allowed Rahahman to meet with the elite citizens of numerous eastern cities including Washington, Baltimore, Philadelphia, New York, and Boston. By 1829, Rahahman achieved his goal of liberating his family and returning to Africa. However, upon reaching African soil, Rahahman tossed aside his feigned embrace of Christianity and eagerly returned to his Islamic faith. Needless to say, his unsuspecting American supporters reacted with surprise and chagrin. Indeed, Rahahman succeeded in "puttin' on Ole Massa" in grand but not atypical style. That effective religious chicanery could occur on a quasi-national scale leaves even less doubt about the slaves' ability to do so within the familiar confines of home. In fact, anthropological research demonstrates that many people endorse "elements of Christian cosmology, but . . . [do] so more for reasons of protection and access to resources, than from intellectual commitment."[11] The story of Abdul Rahahman is an excellent example of such a nominal commitment, and his success suggests that he was not alone in adopting that strategy.

Gomez and Diouf follow Austin's lead by reexamining primary data
to locate evidence for Islamic influence and Muslim slaves throughout
the era of slavery. Both authors succeed in their quest. Evidence for
Muslim slaves appears in slave names, runaway slave advertisements,
plantation records, and historical accounts. By focusing on such traditional materials, these scholars remind their fellow historians that the
evidence, though less plentiful, exists to include Islam as a significant
aspect of North American slave religion. In many cases, old sources
must be revisited with fresh eyes in order to recoup the Islamic heritage of American slaves. Gomez effectively demonstrates the potential
of such research through an examination of the Georgia Sea Islands.

It is well known that a nineteenth-century African American slave
from Sapelo Island, Georgia, wrote a manuscript in Arabic. Using this
information, Gomez reinvestigated historic sources for the region
with the sole purpose of determining if there was a significant Muslim
presence on the island during the antebellum period. Gomez's findings are surprising. Muslim or Arabic names commonly appear in records for the South Carolina and Georgia Sea Islands' slave population
throughout the nineteenth century. Early to mid-twentieth-century
interviews of island residents reveal practices that suggest Islamic
worship. For instance, residents recalled observing fellow islanders
kneeling on mats while praying at particular times during the day. As
with Muslims, some slaves utilized prayer beads and head coverings
and also followed strict dietary habits. Others prayed with books that
they kept hidden while not in use. Even today, the members of the
First African Baptist Church on Sapelo Island pray facing east because
the "devil is in the other corner."[12]

Gomez's findings demonstrate a significant and sustained presence
of Islamic beliefs within both the slave and free communities of the
islands. Such evidence not only supports the idea of greater religious
diversity among slaves; it also requires scholars to reevaluate the current interpreted meanings or origins of various recorded objects and
practices. When viewed through the lens of Islam, some data, as with
the First African Baptist Church's prayer habits, might reveal new
or differing interpretations. For instance, Diouf suggests that the
slaves' revolving ring shout worship services might have their origin
in the Arabic word *sha'wt. Sha'wt,* pronounced as "shout," means to

have completed one revolution around the Kaaba. As both religious activities feature counterclockwise motion, Diouf's suggestion seems credible and worthy of further investigation. Similarly, archaeologists have recovered wrought-brass amulets shaped like fists from slave dwellings in Annapolis, Maryland, and around Nashville, Tennessee. Without considering Islam, these "hands" might be identified as Voodoo or hoodoo charms only. However, it should be taken into account that many Muslims use the "Hand of Fatima" to ward off the evil eye. Joao Jose Reis demonstrates the importance of amulets for Muslim slave rebels in nineteenth-century Brazil.[13] Given the connection that Reis established between Brazilian Muslims and amulets, the North American slaves' fondness for such items deserves further investigation for other possible Islamic cultural transmissions. It is this possibility of cultural influence that makes closer study of Muslims in the slave community so important. While none of the authors cited here argues that Islam was the most important religious force among the slaves, all would agree that Muslims constituted a small, distinctive, and influential portion of the slave population throughout the antebellum period.

A more frequently recognized and written-about African-derived religion that survived among the slaves of North America is Voodoo. Voodoo's greater notoriety in part rests on the sensational coverage it receives from the public and press. The images of zombies, lurid dances, and mystical concoctions conjured by Hollywood and novelists have made the existence of Voodoo in America common knowledge as well as a viable tourist attraction. However, Voodoo rightly deserves scholarly attention because it undoubtedly had more followers among the slaves of the United States than did Islam. As a literacy-based faith, Islam struggled to survive in the United States. Without access to Islamic schools and texts, Muslim slaves were hard pressed to pass on their faith to future generations.[14] As a product of Africa's mostly oral culture, Voodoo faced no such barriers to its survival or expansion.

Voodoo is the best example of African Traditional Religious beliefs that survived the forced migration to North America. Voodoo also represents the most highly developed composite religion that developed as a result of the transatlantic slave trade and slavery. The central beliefs of Voodoo are a synthesis of West African religions and Christianity forged by African peoples prior to and during their experiences with slavery. Antebellum Voodoo had a formal pantheon, priesthood, initiation rites, and religious symbols.[15] Therefore, apart from its popular image, the Voodoo practiced by slaves during the slavery era deserves to be considered a coherent religious system.

Voodoo derives its name from the Dahomean religion and word *Vodun*, which literally means deities or gods. Within the religion of Vodun there are many deities and spiritual entities. Like many West African religions, Vodun revolves around the interaction between a distant high God, lesser deities, spirits, ancestral spirits, humans, animals, and inanimate objects. Vodun's particular pantheon emerged out of the introduction of Yoruban, Mahi, and Ketu beliefs into the core of traditional Dahomean religion. This merger of religious ideas occurred because of Dahomey's territorial and economic expansion in West Africa during the seventeenth century.[16] The incorporation of differing ethnic religious beliefs into Vodun reveals how some West African faiths adjusted to periods of cross-cultural contact and conflict. Dahomean Vodun would continue to undergo this process of adaptation and evolution in the multiethnic environment of eighteenth-century Saint-Domingue.

Slave traders brought members of a wide variety of African ethnic groups to the French Caribbean colony of Saint-Domingue, including many slaves from Dahomey. While Dahomean priests assumed dominance over the religious lives of the slaves brought to the French colony on Hispaniola, practitioners of Vodun soon incorporated deities from other African religions into their worship in order to meet the needs and desires of their increasingly diverse following. Thus today Haitian Vodun includes gods from the Nago, Senegalese, Ibo, Minas, Congo, and Angolans. However, while Vodun successfully survived in its New World incarnation, it did not go unchallenged. As a means of justifying the enslavement of Africans, the French, like most European masters, felt obligated to Christianize their bondsmen. Most slaves on Saint-Domingue were baptized into the Catholic Church, offered a modicum of Christian education, and forbidden to practice their traditional faiths. Clever slaves soon learned to mask their continued practice of Haitian Vodun by blending Catholic Christian symbols and ideas into their worship and iconography. For example, Christian saints and their images became the equivalents of African deities. Legba, the Vodun God of communication, became associated with Saint Peter because of the latter's role as gatekeeper within Christianity. The myth of Saint Patrick ridding Ireland of serpents led him to be linked to Damballah, a Vodun God who often appears as a snake.[17] This blending of religious traditions allowed Haitian Vodun to thrive despite its legal prohibition and thereby continue to serve as the slaves' refuge from white physical and cultural domination.

Vodun probably first arrived in the British North American colonies soon after the introduction of slavery and either survived in small enclaves or merged with other faiths via the process outlined above. However, the most significant influx of Vodun—or Voodoo, as it is called in the United States—occurred when African and Afro-Caribbean slaves from Saint-Domingue arrived in the lower Mississippi River region during the Haitian Revolution of the late eighteenth century. Many of the masters fleeing the slave rebellion on Hispaniola relocated themselves and their slaves to Louisiana. The city of New Orleans subsequently functioned as the religious center for Voodoo worship, but its influence radiated outward to many of the plantations located along the Mississippi River. Some reports even suggest that during the nineteenth century, Voodoo worship occurred as far north as Missouri.[18]

Following the 1803 purchase of Louisiana by the United States, Voodoo continued to survive among believers. The secret to the vitality of Voodoo lay in the religion's ability to address the everyday needs of slaves. Voodoo priestesses and priests, often African born, could offer believers healing powers when they were sick, corrective measures for life's everyday difficulties, and protection against those that would hurt them. In other words, Voodoo was an extremely practical religion that gained further legitimacy by having its roots in African rather than white tradition. These attributes allowed Voodoo practitioners to be so successful in pursuing their faith that several of their religious leaders held tremendous sway within the New Orleans community. Sanite Dede and the two Marie Laveaus are generally considered to be the most notable of these leaders. Today, the power of Voodoo still resonates in and around New Orleans as well as other major metropolitan areas throughout the country.[19] Such longevity is a tribute to the strength of the slaves' desire and ability to maintain their African faiths.

While Islam and Voodoo certainly preceded and coexisted with Christianity among the southern slave population, neither faith could be considered as representative of African Americans as a whole. A majority of the slaves most likely created and practiced new composite religions rather than being strict adherents to any of the above faiths. Despite a general lack of support for this idea among slavery historians, there is solid evidence to support the plausibility of such an interpretation.

As previously discussed, numerous scholars of slave and African Traditional Religion argue that African tribal faiths share many common elements. Religion historian Edward Geoffrey Parrinder uses the words "comparative homogeneity" to describe the vast "religious sphere" of African society. While Sidney W. Mintz and Richard Price do not view western and central Africa as a unified cultural area, they too argue that the regions' cultures share "grammatical principles" that provide "basic assumptions about social relations . . . and expectations about the way the world functions phenomenologically." Will Coleman identifies numerous religious characteristics that he describes as being part of a "West African cosmos." John S. Mbiti helps explain these similarities by noting that as African Traditional Religion must "meet the needs of the time," it has to be flexible. Therefore, "change did come upon African Religion from place to place, and from time to time, through leading personalities of the nation, the intermingling of peoples, and natural necessities." In other words, cultural sharing and adaptation were common among the peoples of Africa, especially during times of contact and conflict.[20] In the Caribbean, such circumstances produced the West African religious synthesis called Voodoo. In all probability, the forced migration of differing African peoples to mainland North America yielded a few similar creations of its own.

Michael A. Gomez argues as much when he writes that by the 1830s "African religions were still practiced by a majority [of slaves], with some transformation of meaning, along with the incorporation of a few tenets of the Christian faith." This interpretation squares with the findings of Emefie Ikenga-Metuh, who argues that Africans are more likely to incorporate new forms of worship into a traditional pantheon than to accept monolatry or monotheism. It may help explain the strange union of Denmark Vesey's Charleston African Church allies and the crab-claw-adorned soldiers of Gullah Jack. Furthermore, pseudo-conversions by persons incorporating Christian elements into their lives are documented elsewhere in North America. For example, the Spanish Catholic priests sent to what they believed was the converted native population of the Yucatan Peninsula were shocked by the Mayans' religious practices. The priests discovered that the Mayan "Christians" of the Yucatan combined Christian iconography with their traditional religious practice of human sacrifice.[21]

In the words of Charles H. Long, "The slaves did not confront America with a religious tabula rasa." Africans retained the memory of their native faiths even though their new environs undermined their attachment to a specific spiritual community and limited their ability to engage in traditional ritual. These conditions forced Africans and their descendants to find common ground with their fellow bondsmen of different ethnicities. It would be these areas of common ground that "served as a catalyst in the processes by which individuals from diverse societies forged new institutions, and . . . provided certain frameworks within which new [religious] forms could have developed." As with the development of pidgin languages, early composite religions contained limited "spiritual vocabularies" that centered on the most basic needs of the emerging slave community. While this process likely eliminated complex pantheons and nuanced theology, it did allow for the development of a shared spiritual worldview and rituals centering on daily concerns like protection, interpersonal relations, and the appeasement of the dearly departed. In time the community's "spiritual vocabulary" grew as social interaction bred innovations reflecting local conditions. As parents passed their adapted beliefs on to their children, the earlier pidgin form of their faith became creolized and served as the native belief system of the community.[22]

This is not to suggest that most slaves possessed a singular coherent faith with widespread theological integrity. Isolated plantations and farms with irregular interregional communication precluded such developments and allowed for regional or local religious patterns to emerge that greatly reflected the cultures of the Africans brought to that part of the United States. W. E. B. Du Bois described this religious tradition as "not at first by any means Christian nor definitely organized; rather it was an adaptation and mingling of heathen rites among the members of each plantation." Thus, the dispersed southern settlement pattern created distinctive regional identities that allowed Upper South slaves to consider the practices of Louisiana and Sea Island bondsmen strange and vice versa. However, as with the emergence of the Christian core, the steady influence of westward migration undoubtedly allowed for further blending and the muting of religious differences among the slaves. Regional differences aside, what these various communities of slaves practiced was nonetheless religion and religion based largely on similar, if not shared, African concepts.[23]

Although very few slaves were willing to discuss the African religious beliefs of their communities, this does not mean that evidence of these beliefs does not exist. The narrative of Charles Ball describes both the existence of Muslim slaves and followers of some forms of African Traditional Religion. As discussed in an earlier chapter, Ball informs his readers that his grandfather "had singular religious notions—never going to meeting or caring for the preachers he could, if he would, occasionally hear. He retained his native traditions respecting the Deity and hereafter." Ball also points out that his grandfather was not alone in maintaining his lifelong religious beliefs. The chapter-opening quotation from Charles Ball vividly recounts his participation in helping two parents bury their child according to African religious practices. Frederick Douglass recalled a slave named Sandy who "was not only a religious man, but he professed to believe in a system for which I have no name. He was a genuine African, and had inherited some of the so-called magical powers said to be possessed by eastern nations." Methodist missionaries described slaves in Alabama and South Carolina who were "still clinging to the darkness and superstition of . . . greegree worship" or "whose sole religious ideas consisted of crying to the sun and moon when they arose." C. C. Jones agreed with this assessment and noted, "The superstitions brought from Africa have not been wholly laid aside." Even those attempting to applaud the mission efforts to the slaves admitted that older religious ideals still dominated the African American community. In the 1859 biography of missionary William Capers, author William May Wightman admitted that efforts to convert the slaves met with only slight success because "[a] great deal of ignorance has been in the way, on the part of the old negroes; many superstitious notions, many fixed habits of immorality, have opposed barriers to the entrance of the word of God to the inner man. The improvement on the part of the younger generation has not been as extensive as their opportunities of instruction."[24] In other words, as late as two years prior to the Civil War, traditional religious beliefs continued to thrive even in areas where Christians had actively worked to convert the slaves for at least thirty years.

Research from the field of archaeology provides significant additional evidence of the continuation of African-based religions within the United States' slave population. In recent years, archaeologists have identified Colono Ware, an unglazed, low-fired, plain earthenware pottery, as an important indicator of the vitality of African cultural traditions in the New World. Colono Ware regularly appears at seventeenth-, eighteenth-, and nineteenth-century slave sites, ranging from the Chesapeake Bay to the St. Johns River of northeast Florida. Archaeologists originally attributed Colono Ware to Native American craftsmen. However, archaeologist Leland G. Ferguson has since shown that Colono Ware is also a New World continuation of an ancient West African pottery tradition. A comparison between recovered forms of Colono Ware and excavated examples of West African pottery revealed that the ceramic forms are remarkably similar. In fact, the two artifacts used could not be differentiated without performing a detailed compositional analysis of their paste and temper.[25]

The linkage between the existence of slave-made Colono Ware and the continuance of African religions turns on the appearance of markings found on recovered pottery. In particular, an incised "X" or cross frequently appears on the base or surface of Colono Ware bowls. This symbol also commonly appears on pottery vessels manufactured in West African Ghana and on knives and spoons recovered from slave sites in North Carolina and Virginia. The symbol's consistent appearance and wide geographical presence suggests that it is not a maker's mark.[26] Leland G. Ferguson argues that as the symbol closely resembles Kongo cosmograms, it is probably a religious symbol. A brief description of the history and meaning behind Kongo cosmograms helps illustrate this assertion.

The Bakongo are an African people traditionally inhabiting western Zaire, a region heavily favored by slave traders. Among the Bakongo, "philosophers explain the earth, the land of the living, as a mountain over a watery barrier separating this world from the land of the dead beneath. Each day the sun rises over the earth and proceeds in a counterclockwise direction . . . across the sky to set in the water . . . [where] during earthly nighttime, the sun illuminates the underside of the universe, the land of the dead, until it rises again in the northeast."[27] Thus, according to Ferguson, the incised "X" on the bowls is a visual representation of the spiritual intersection of the land of the living and the land of the dead.

The spiritual emphasis that Bakongo religion places on water offers significant support to this interpretation of Colono Ware pottery. Of the countless examples of Colono Ware vessels found throughout the South, 75 percent of the "X"-marked artifacts have been located underwater. Interestingly, many of the "X"-marked Colono Ware vessels found there are completely intact or largely unscathed. The good condition of these underwater pieces of Colono Ware leads Ferguson to interpret that they were not discarded as trash. Rather, Ferguson argues, African Americans deliberately placed these Colono Ware pieces into their watery depositories, suggesting their use in religious rituals of a non-Christian nature.[28]

Ferguson's theory gains additional support from the frequent recovery of unusual objects of personal adornment from excavated slave sites. Many of these recovered pieces provide tangible evidence of religious diversity among the United States' slave population. Indeed, since Robert Ascher and Charles H. Fairbanks' pioneering archaeological efforts on Cumberland Island, Georgia, blue beads have been conspicuous among recovered slave artifacts. Beads similar to these have traditionally been used as charms in both Africa and the Middle East to ward off the "evil eye." In fact, as "[o]bjects of spiritual efficacy, charms were greatly valued by Africans for the health, protection, and prosperity of the individual and the community." Other unexplained items that regularly appear at slave sites leave further room for expanding the range of artifacts tied to religious beliefs or ritual. Among these items are cowrie shells, pierced coins, prisms, and ebony rings.[29]

Archaeological evidence for the diversity of slave religion is not lim-

ited to marked pottery vessels and objects of personal adornment. Pol-
ished stones, reworked glass and ceramic pieces, and Native American
points found at numerous African American sites indicate the slaves'
use of *minkisi,* spiritual medicines needed to manipulate the spiritual
realm. "Minkisi are the literal dwelling places for the spirit and personalities of the dead. They function as portable shrines, and serve a
key role in African Bakongo religion." Likewise, Kenneth Brown and
Doreen Cooper unearthed an assemblage of "ritual paraphernalia" on
the Jordan Plantation near Houston, Texas, that also suggests the
practice of divination or non-Western healing techniques. In particular, excavation of the Jordan's nineteenth-century slave and tenant
farmer quarters yielded "cast-iron kettles, pieces of used chalk, bird
skulls, fragments of a weighing scale, an animal's paw, samples of medicine, sea shells, bottles, and chert scrapers." Brown and Cooper show
that this assemblage resembles the ritual tool kits that West Africans
traditionally use for divination. A similar find in Annapolis, Maryland,
demonstrates that such religious persistence was not limited to slaves
living in isolated, rural locations but could also take place within an
urban setting.[30] The appearance of these objects suggests that many
African American slaves retained their belief in some form of an African-based religion.

The best evidence for the widespread practice of some modified
form of African Traditional Religion is the slaves' ubiquitous belief
in conjure and spirits. According to Mechal Sobel, "No slave area was
without spirit-workers, and virtually no slave was without contact with
spirits." Many scholars label these elements of slave culture as simply
folk beliefs or superstitions that survived apart from their original
religious context. However, in *Black Culture and Black Consciousness,*
Lawrence W. Levine rightly describes these elements of slave culture
as "religious beliefs." Eugene D. Genovese is more cautious in his assessment but nonetheless argues that "Southern black 'superstition,'
on closer inspection, takes on the attributes of a folk religion." Charles
W. Joyner boldly asserts that "conjuration and sorcery flourished as
an underground alternative religious system." Charles E. Orser elabo-
rates on this point by declaring that conjure reflected "a unified version of several religions" that resulted from the slaves' rejection of "all
but their traditional religions . . . and their traditional cosmology."[31]

Such interpretations make sense given the significant role that religio-magical rites played in the African faiths slaves carried to the New World. "For most Africans . . . belief in a supreme being or beings was peripheral rather than central to religious life; the creator or creators inspired less awe than apathy and the aim of religious life was, not to commune with spiritual beings, but to explain, predict and control worldly events." In fact, in many African religions it is the emphasis on explanation, prediction, and control of worldly events that serves as the "basic sustainer of religious life." Many slaves also attributed the conjurers' mystical powers to a deity or supernatural forces that govern the universe. Thus, conjure and the slaves' frequent interaction with the spirit realm was not folk activity devoid of religious significance. Yvonne P. Chireau asserts that African American religion and magic are "complementary categories" and that "permutations of the supernatural in practices such as conjuring . . . have been resignified as 'religion.'" Indeed, these beliefs reflect an adaptation and continuance of African religious practices that helped organize the slaves' community and explain their world.[32]

If one accepts Edwin S. Gaustad's definition of folk religion, there can be no other way to describe these beliefs than to call them religious in nature. According to Gaustad, "[I]n all folk religions, one finds myth (something believed) and ritual (something done)." These two pillars of folk religion explain "that which lies beyond science and before history, probes for that which is true not for one time and place but for all time and all space," and provides ceremonies that "call upon all of the resources and accumulated tradition of the group in order to guide the perplexed, comfort the afflicted, and strengthen those who could not make life's journey alone."[33] Clearly, the slaves' ideas and practices that many label as folk beliefs served these very specific religious functions.

Slaves lived in a world in which contact with spirits was common, accepted, and expected. Lawrence W. Levine eloquently argues that this was so because the slaves, like their African ancestors, believed that

Man was part of, not alien to, the Natural Order of things, attached to the Oneness that bound all matter, animate and inanimate, all spirits, visible or not. It was crucially necessary to understand the world because one was part of it, inexorably linked to it. Survival and happiness and health depended upon being able to read signs that existed everywhere, to understand the visions that recurrently visited one, to commune with the spirits that filled the world: the spirit of the Supreme Being who could be approached only through the spirits of the pantheon of the intermediary deities; the spirits of all the matter that filled the universe—trees, animals, rivers, the very utensils and weapons upon which Man was dependent; the spirits of contemporary human beings; the spirits of ancestors who linked the living world with the unseen world.[34]

Former slaves routinely described the inherited spiritual world their community inhabited. Thomas Johnson declared, "Superstition is characteristic of the race in Africa. . . . [I]t was natural we should retain the superstitions of our fathers." Charles Ball observed, "[T]he negroes of the cotton plantations are exceedingly superstitious; and they are indeed prone, beyond all other people that I have ever known, to believe in ghosts, and the existence of an infinite number of supernatural agents." William Grimes admitted to believing in witches, hearing ghosts groan, and witnessing how "the spirits would unlock the doors, and come up stairs, and trample on me, press me to the floor, and squeeze me almost to death." Henry Cheatam described experiences with multiple ghostly creatures and declared "dere is good and bad spirits." Patsy Mitchner asserted that "our spirits is always wanderin' even before we dies. Spirits is wanderin' eberywhere an' you has to look out for 'em." Ellen Trell, who believed in witches and spells, concurs with Mitchner in remembering how her suffering mother once groaned "go away, evil spirit, go away." Like many former slaves, Sam Rawls described having his sleep disrupted on account of being ridden by a witch. For those who doubted such experiences, M. E. Abrams protested, "T'aint no use fer white folks to low dat it ain't no haints, an' grievements dat follow ye all around, kaise I is done had too many 'spriences wide dem."[35] Placed within Gaustad's definition, the slaves' spiritual world clearly comprised a shared general mythology that many astute observers acknowledged.

These beliefs allowed the slaves to understand their own and their ancestors' place within the universe. All humans, like all creatures, lived, then died, only to live again in an invisible, earthly spirit world as created by a distant but powerful creator. John C. Brown hints at such a view in acknowledging a belief in "a Great Spirit," denying the existence of "hell and everlastin' brimstone," and believing that good and bad people are transformed into entities reflective of their past behavior. That most others probably followed Christians in calling their supreme being or Great Spirit "God" is inconsequential. "God" is the most commonly used word in the English language to describe a supreme being. In the transition from African languages to English, the word "God" undoubtedly served as a unifying and camouflaging replacement for the diverse descriptors that different African tribes had originally given to their creator deity. Simply put, the names changed but the cosmology remained virtually the same. C. C. Jones argued as much when describing the religious practices of Muslim slaves in Georgia. According to Jones, "The Mohammedan Africans remaining of the old stock of importations, although accustomed to hear the Gospel preached, have been known to accommodate Christianity to Mohammedanism. 'God,' say they, 'is Allah, and Jesus Christ is Mohammed—the religion is the same, but different countries have different names.'"[36]

The slaves' interaction with the spiritual world also gave them ritual. They relied on signs from nature to explain or anticipate events and performed specific rites to shape life's outcome. When in doubt of their own power to do so effectively or of the proper corrective measures to employ, slaves commonly consulted conjurers and hoodoo doctors, their priesthood, to direct or combat the spirit or spirits in question. Williams Wells Brown recalled that belief in ghosts, "Voudooism," "goopherism," and fortune-telling had an exalted place within the slave community. Louis Hughes described belief in conjure as "very generally and tenaciously held to by all classes" among the slaves. Henry Bibb admitted, "There is much superstition among the slaves. Many of them believe in what they call 'conjuration, tricking, and witchcraft.'" Frederick Douglass acknowledged that the belief in root work was "very common." Likewise, Henry Bruce could "remember the time when a large majority of them believed strongly in all kinds of superstition voodooism, gophering, tricking and conjuring."[37]

By possessing the knowledge of proper ritual, the conjurer, like the Voodoo priest, served "as the healer of the sick, the interpreter of the Unknown, the comforter of the sorrowing, [and] the supernatural avenger of the wrong." Folklorists have collected volumes of these rituals that, much like the Christian Ten Commandments, provided the slaves with guidelines for safe and proper living. For example, Jenny Proctor remembered slaves wearing lead bullets, asafetida balls, and rabbit's feet to "keep off evil of any kind." As a young man, Frederick Douglass famously carried a root given to him to protect himself from a brutal overseer. Likewise, Louis Hughes described how "it was the custom" for slaves to carry "voo-doo bags" containing "roots, nuts, pins and some other things" to protect themselves from being whipped. Silvia Witherspoon sought protection from supernatural torments. Witherspoon kept a flour sifter and a fork by her bed to prevent her from being ridden by witches. Others used conjure ritual to attain their desires or shape their environment. Henry Pyles, like many other young people, bought a "hand" to woo the lover of his choice. George Leonard recalled that the old people could use conjure rites to "punish anybody."[38]

These rituals and the accompanying folklore served as a means of asserting and protecting communal values. "When an individual . . . strayed far enough from the group's acceptable behavior, they [were] fixed." In this way, the community of believers maintained order both within their human and spiritual relationships. In fact, these beliefs were so important to the slaves that Philip D. Morgan writes that "[t]he religious worldview of early American slaves was primarily magical, not Christian." W. E. B. Du Bois seconds Morgan's interpretation by describing "the witch-woman and the voodoo-priest . . . [as] the centre of Negro group life." Christian missionaries recognized this and considered conjurers to be not only an impediment to slave conversion but their chief competitors for the religious attention of the slaves. C. C. Jones decried the power of the conjurer over their community in noting that slaves "have not dared to disobey him in the least particular . . . notwithstanding all other influences brought to bear upon them." William Capers even made a special effort to expel a suspected witch from his class meetings because of the power his parishioners believed she had over them.[39]

This animated spiritual worldview, which exemplifies the continuation of various forms of African Traditional Religion within the antebellum slave community, is also reflected in African American funerary practices. The work of Robert L. Hall as well as that of Sylvia R. Frey and Betty Wood reveals that slaves often followed the practice of second burial. Second burial is an Ibo communal celebration that occurs sometime after the initial interment of the body and protects the deceased's family from being "harassed and victimized by the hovering restless spirit of the dead person." George Brandon found that, as in Africa, some slaves considered animal sacrifice and food offerings as indispensable aspects of a proper funeral. Likewise, the works of John Vlach and Robert Thompson demonstrate that African religious beliefs dominated slave concepts of death. Slaves often decorated graves with common household objects or personal items of the deceased. Cups, saucers, mirrors, bottles, clocks, and seashells are among the items frequently found on old African American graves. These items either served as a form of minkisi that directed the spirit to his or her final destination or provided the deceased with needed items for use in the spirit world. More important, second burial, sacrifices, and grave gifts also served as an incentive for the dead to remain satisfied in death and not to wander about among the living as a malevolent spirit.[40]

Such actions demonstrate that the belief in the interactive bond between the living and the dead common to many African religions continued to influence the behavior and mind-set of the slaves. Of equal significance is the fact that these ideas clearly lay outside the Christian tradition of most nineteenth-century Americans. The idea that a living person can influence the fate of the deceased is not part of the Protestant Christianity typical of most of the former slaveholding regions of the United States. Undoubtedly, evangelical Protestants would reject the notion that one's condition in the afterlife could be determined by anyone other than the individual concerned. Indeed, evangelicals emphasize the Bible's pronouncement that one achieves salvation by God's grace and not by specific human works.[41] Clearly, evangelical Christians of the antebellum era would not have taught or accepted the notion that earthly actions or works could influence one's experience in the afterlife. This suggests that the slaves' actions represent the influence of African religious practices that recalled traditional aspects of ancestor veneration and spirit appeasement.

What is striking about these religious retentions is that even members of the slave Christian core adhered to many of these beliefs despite their falling outside of Christian orthodoxy. On this point, Albert J. Raboteau argues that "[c]onjure could, without contradiction, exist side by side with Christianity in the same individual and in the same community because, for the slaves, conjure answered purposes which Christianity did not and Christianity answered purposes which conjure did not."[42] Yvonne P. Chireau does not separate conjure from Christianity like Raboteau but, as previously mentioned, views them as "complementary categories." Chireau's work demonstrates that many slaves embraced and interwove Christianity and the conjure spirit world into the meaning of their daily lives.[43] This melding of conjure and the slaves' spiritual worldview with Christianity is what made Afro-Christianity the highly distinctive form of the faith that is so well documented.[44] Most slaves had only limited access to thoroughly orthodox Christian doctrine as they were denied literacy, frequently instructed via a simplified catechism, and given irregular access to trained clergy. As a result, slave Christians attempted to worship their God through age-old methods of engaging the spiritual realm. New Christian converts carried into their new faith long-standing communal experience with mystical events like religious trances and spirit possession. C. C. Jones was dismayed by this and complained that slave Christians found "true conversion, in dreams, visions, trances, voices—all bearing a perfect or striking resemblance to some form or type which has been handed down for generations."[45] It was these old traditions that led the Christian core to combine sacred movement/dance and prayer in the form of the ring shout. Similarly, in one Methodist service the tradition of spirit possession undoubtedly moved "Aunt Katy" to gesticulate wildly and declare that she was the incarnation of the "young King Jesus." Katy's behavior came as a great shock to Reverend Joseph Travis, who promptly removed her from the service before readmitting her to the congregation at a later date once she "became a rational and consistent member of the Church."[46]

Such worship forms within Afro-Christianity clearly demonstrate the blending of an African spiritual worldview with Christianity. However, they also reveal just how deeply rooted and important these beliefs were within the community at large. Slave Christians embraced the "whites' religion," but many also held onto earlier religious values that kept them firmly rooted within the broader slave community. In other words, while the "sinners" went to the frolics when the Christians attended prayer meetings, many slaves from both camps acknowledged the power of haunts and witches and depended on the skills of the conjurer. This was particularly true as conjure was frequently appealed to as a defense against slaveholders. In the words of W. E. B. Du Bois, the slave viewed bondage as "the dark triumph of Evil over him." To combat this evil, slaves "called up all the resources of heathenism to aid,—exorcism and witchcraft, the mysterious Obi worship with its barbarous rites, spells, and blood sacrifice."[47] By retaining this aspect of their mutual struggle, slave Christians who practiced conjure diminished the division that existed between Christians and non-Christians and helped them achieve greater unity by reminding them of their common oppressors. If the survey data and evidence of conversion barriers are credible, then I would suggest that conjure beliefs, rather than Christianity, were more commonly the glue that held the slave community together.

Deciding where the conjure faiths ended and Christianity began is tricky business, however. The syncretistic practices of Afro-Christians place most of the slaves' religious beliefs on a continuum between African Traditional Religion and orthodox Christianity; this prevents the positioning of a dividing line between the two endpoints. As shown earlier, slaves could and did differentiate between Christian and non-Christian members of their community, using personal insights and experiences to do so. One can safely assume that slave Christians would have expected fellow believers to identify Jesus Christ as the primary spiritual intermediary in their lives. However, beyond that, their criteria for inclusion in or exclusion from the Christian community continue to elude modern scholars. Did using a Bible in a conjure ritual reveal one's primary faith in Christianity, or was it a perversion of the Gospel that made one an infidel or a heretic at best? We shall never truly know. This complicates the argument presented here and prevents a truly precise calculation of the size of the Christian and conjure faith communities. Yet it is clear that most slaves embraced the remnants of an African spiritual worldview and at least some ele-

ments of conjure, be they Christian or non-Christian. Thus the religious outlook of most slaves who fell along the aforementioned spiritual continuum would have been influenced by these ideals.

Not all of the Christian core embraced this compromise between
their ancestral worldview and Christianity, however. Many recognized
the incompatibility of these beliefs with orthodox Christianity and
registered their disdain for those who continued to embrace the faith
of the conjure priests as members of the church. Ank Bishop stated
that "dis here voodoo an' hoodoo an' sper'ts ain't nothin' but a lot of
folk's outten Christ." Elizabeth Hite told how her congregation rejected a slave woman because "she was the biggest rascal and worstest
witch on the plantation. . . . It was too late to save her. She was really a
lost soul, heavy wit' sin and bound for Hell." Sara Brown heard people
speaking about conjure but didn't "pay no attention to dey talk" because " [d]at de devil work en I ain' bother wid it." James Boyd avoided
conjure out of fear for his very soul. Boyd admitted to interviewers
that "deres spirits an sech an I has talked wif de witch doctors, but
it ain't fer twel de light gwine shone ober yonder fer dis nigger an I
ain't gwine to think of sech. . . . I ain't gwine have no doin' wid no sech
truck." Finally, Martha Colquitt remembered that her grandmother
and mother "told us chillun voodoo wuz a no 'count doin' of de devil,
and Christians wuz never to pay it no 'tention."[48]

The rejection of the conjurer's spirit-filled world by orthodox slave
Christians was a portent of things to come. The Christian core had
long prophesied about the coming of freedom. Emancipation demonstrated the power of the Christian God and gave those within the
Christian core who criticized conjure new and substantial credibility.
With the coming of freedom, this unchained force grew dramatically
as ever-greater numbers of African Americans found solace and celebration in Christianity. As a result, freedom would deliver dramatic religious change within the slave community as an old order faded while
another rose in triumph.

❦ 4 ❦
CHRIST UNCHAINED

If you hold to my teaching, you are really my disciples. Then you will know the truth, and the truth will set you free.
—JOHN 8:31–32

I tell you chile, it was pitiful, but God did not let it last always. I have heard slaves morning and night pray for deliverance. Some of 'em would stand up in de fields or bend over cotton and corn and pray out loud for God to help 'em and in time you see, He did.
—CLAYBORN GANTLING, in Rawick, *American Slave*

Given the numerous barriers to conversion and the inadequacy of the South's missionary efforts, it is a wonder that as many African Americans converted as did. C. C. Jones attributed many of these conversions to the fact that African Americans "preach[ed] the Gospel to each other." Indeed, the Christian core's religious fervor and faithfulness to Christianity made them a dynamic force for conversion within the slave community. This small but devoted segment of the southern African American population willingly faced the threat of physical punishment and even death in order to pursue their faith. Christianity gave these believers spiritual relief from the everyday pain of slavery and hope for a better world to come. Most slave Christians also believed that God would ultimately provide them with earthly freedom when the time was right. Slaves regularly but quietly prophesied and prayed about the day when God would break the shackles of bondage and set his righteous people free. When that anticipated deliverance arrived, slave Christians stood as a people justified in their faith and served as the greatest testament of their God's power.[1] The Christian core's faithfulness and accuracy in anticipating emancipation thereby attracted ever-greater numbers of African American freedmen to Christianity. Freedom, rather than slavery, proved the greatest force for conversion among African Americans in the South.

Slaveholders routinely attempted to shape the slaves' religious experiences in ways that favored white rather than African American needs. These efforts to retain control ranged from prohibiting any religious services to dictating sermon content or allowing only family prayer meetings. Failure to comply with these restrictions often led to the banning of all religious services, physical punishment, or even death for slave Christians. William Williams of North Carolina recalled that his overseer "would whip a slave if he found him praying." Mary James's Virginia master sold her grandfather south for being religious and praying that God would set the slaves free. The master of Thomas H. Jones swore that if he did not abandon religion, "I will whip you to death." While Jones's master ultimately stopped short of murdering Thomas, the sister of John Andrew Jackson paid the ultimate price for her religious principles. She died at the hands of her cruel mistress because she refused to quit praying in spite of several previous warnings to do so. Yet, despite such real dangers, slave Christians persisted in worshiping their God according to the dictates of their heart. One Louisiana slave even commented that such persecution made African American believers better Christians. He argued that when slave Christians faced little opposition, "[a]ll quiet, den all grow cold, and dey follers de Lord afar off." In contrast, when slave owners fought slave prayers with punishment or death, "all these troubles and trials dey drives us to de Lord."[2] These comments, while unique to this individual, testify to the great dedication many bondsmen had for their faith.

Christian slaves refused to abandon their faith because its teachings gave them an identity and future that they could embrace fully. Specifically, Christianity asserts the value of all human beings, whether they are black or white or slave or free. The teachings of Jesus indicate that all individuals are an important part of the Christian God's creation. No one, no matter how lowly in earthly status, is worth less than another person in the eyes of God. All humans are children of God and equally subject to his commandments. The Christian God even sacrificed his only son in order to offer eternal life to every individual who accepts and follows his teachings. Furthermore, Christian theology promises that this gift of eternal life will take place in a heavenly existence of divine justice and peace.[3]

Each of these emphases of the Christian religion would have had great meaning for slave converts. Christianity's respect for the value of humanity must have had special significance for individuals who found themselves appraised and sold like livestock. The idea of spiritual equality and uniform moral standards had to appeal to persons legally defined as inferior and subjected to the capricious justice of southern slave codes. Having lost family members to sale or premature death, African American slaves could also fully appreciate the Christian God's sacrifice of his only son on their behalf. Finally, the promise of a better world to come undoubtedly would appeal to persons whose earthly existence was primarily rigorous labor enforced by real or potential violence.

While the Christian core certainly looked forward to heaven, eternal salvation was not their only goal. Slave Christians took hold of the biblical story of the ancient Israelites' exodus from slavery in Egypt and made it their own. As Albert J. Raboteau argues, this linkage with Israel "gave the slaves a communal identity as a special, divinely favored people" and foretold of their future deliverance. Slave believers spoke to one another about their anticipated freedom and made it a common feature in their sermons and prayers. James Williams recalled a devout Christian named Solomon who reacted calmly to ill treatment by his overseer. When asked how he could tolerate such treatment, Solomon replied that "it would not always be so—that slavery was to come to an end for the Bible said so." Mingo White believed that the slaves "had a instinct dat we was goin' to be free" and as a result frequently prayed "for de Lawd to free dem lack he did de chillun of Is'ael." According to Robert J. Cheatham, "The negro preachers preached freedom into our ears and our old men and women prophecied about it." Finally, Victoria Perry's mother routinely awakened her by praying and saying, "Someday we are going to be free: the Good Lord won't let this thing go on all the time."[4]

When slave Christians learned about the Confederate assault on Fort Sumter, many predicted, accurately, that the time of their deliverance was at hand. As a result, throughout the war, an increasing number of slaves lifted petitions to God for southern defeat and the end of slavery. Former Georgia slave Mary Gladdy remembered that during the war slaves gathered for prayer meetings because "[t]heir great, soul hungering desire was freedom." On the plantation where Maria Heywood lived, such prayer meetings occurred "[a]ll bout in people house. Hold the four year of the war." Once Ebenezer Brown's masters left for the war, "All de time dey wus gone de slaves kept prayin' to be sot free." During the wartime prayer meetings she attended, Channa Littlejohn remembered specific petitions asking for the Yankees to come. Such prayer meetings were so common during the war that some whites sought to prevent their occurrence lest the slaves' prayers come true. Callie Williams pointed out that "[d]ey tried to make 'em stop singin' and prayin' durin' de war" because whites knew "all dey'd ask for was to be set free." Williams goes on to say that white attempts to stop these meetings were unsuccessful. In fact, according to Tom Robinson, despite white attempts to prohibit these heavenly petitions, "[a]ll over the country the same prayer was being prayed."[5]

With the war over and freedom secured, most former slaves had little doubt about who was responsible for their deliverance. Many freedmen, like Mingo White and Robert J. Cheatham, stated that "Abraham Lincoln was the agent of the true and living God" sent to deliver his people from bondage. Others like O. W. Green and Clayborn Gantling emphasized that "[t]was only because of de prayers of de cullud people, dey was freed." Former Louisiana slave Charlotte Brooks gave multiple credit for the coming of emancipation. Brooks believed that "[w]e done the praying and the Yankees done the fighting, and God heard our prayers 'way down here in these cane-fields." Some freedmen, like L. M. Mills of St. Louis, proved eloquent in their analysis of emancipation. Mills noted that it was "[n]o wonder God sent war on this nation! It was the old story of the captivity in Egypt repeated. The slaveholders were warned time and again to let the black man go, but they hardened their hearts and would not, until finally the wrath of God was poured out upon them and the sword of the great North fell upon their first born." Regardless of what spin freedmen gave to their newfound freedom, most identified the Christian God as the ultimate source of their deliverance. This was true even for some individuals who were previously skeptical about the Christian core's expectation of freedom. One freedman admitted, "I've heard them pray for freedom. I thought it was foolishness then, but the old time folks always felt they was to be free. It must have been something 'vealed unto 'em."[6] Thus, freedmen commonly viewed emancipation as either the fulfillment of biblical promise or as the answer to decades of prayer. In either case, the rewarded faithfulness of the slave Christian core drew thousands of previously skeptical African Americans to Christianity. Where slavery had once barred the door to Christian salvation, freedom allowed the multitude to enter God's kingdom unobstructed.

Freedmen vividly remembered the dramatic impact that the Civil War and emancipation had on their religious lives. Many recalled increased religious activity among the newly freed, while others spoke of their conversion as a result of war-related events. For instance, Mollie Edmonds recalled, "After surrender us held meetings in big tents and had a preacher, what could tell us the word of God. Before that, there wasn't much Christianity amongst us." Virginian Julia Williams noted that "[d]e slaves had more meetin's and gatherin's aftah de war." Henry Baker exclaimed, "We served de Lawd sho nuff aftuh we wuz sot free cause we had sumpin tuh be thankful for. Aftuh Surrender [sic], 'niggers' dey sung, dey prayed, dey preached." Harriett Gresham recalled that upon emancipation, "One and all they remembered to thank God for their freedom. They immediately began to hold meetings, singing soul stirring spirituals." According to Charlie Robinson, "When freedom come. . . [d]at year us all jined de church."[7] It is interesting to note that in Gresham and Robinson's description of events after the Civil War, the antebellum division between the Christian core and nonbelievers seems to have disappeared. This suggests that for some freedmen, the war forged, at least temporarily, a unified religious community centered on giving thanks to the Christian God.

Freedmen who fought as soldiers during the Civil War also remembered emancipation as being crucial to their commitment to Christianity. After serving in the Union Army, Barney Stone became a preacher out of "gratefulness to God for my deliverance and my salvation." Another Union veteran credited his conversion to the fact that God had protected him during the war and thus it was appropriate to trust in him after his discharge. Tennessean Julius Jones "had never tended a real service before . . . I was grown . . . [but] got religion while I was in one of those war hospitals." Finally, white Union soldier Zenas T.

Haines recalled hearing African American soldiers seeking conversion while camped in New Bern, North Carolina. As Haines noted in his diary, "Our nights are rendered musical by the plaintive choral hymnings of devotional negroes in every direction, alone and in groups. From their open cabins come the mingled voices of men wrestling painfully and agonizingly with the spirit, and those uttering the ecstatic notes of the unredeemed."[8] Haines's observation is significant not only because it helps demonstrate a general tendency for African American conversion during the Civil War but because it also suggests a specific change in the pattern of male conversion. According to the statistical study outlined in chapter 1, male adult slaves were the least likely segment of the slave population to convert to Christianity. However, released from bondage and allowed to fight their oppressors, African American males sought conversion in sufficient numbers to dominate the sounds heard in an army encampment.

Haines was not alone in detecting an increase in Christian conversions among African Americans during and after the Civil War. James Mallory, an Alabama slave owner and deeply religious man, made several observations concerning the religious condition of African Americans in his community between the years 1862 and 1868. On August 17, 1862, Mallory noted in his journal that "a revival is in progress amongst our blacks, a number were added to the church and baptised." Later that year Mallory continued to note an increase in the number of conversions among the slave population. On October 19, Mallory wrote, "[T]heir [sic] is quite a revival amongst the servants, from twenty eyght [sic] to thirty were baptized today." After emancipation Mallory became disturbed by the intensity of the freedmen's increased religious feelings: "Religious excitement amongst the freedmen has become alarming, they seem falling fast into idoletry [sic]. . . . [T]he negroes have almost quit work, waiting for the judgement to come in a few days." While one might interpret Mallory's observations as the bitter commentary of a slave owner stung by emancipation, this does not appear to have been the case. Mallory, while frustrated by the South's stumbling steps toward free labor, was not critical in his general remarks about the freedmen. In fact, just a few days before expressing concern about the religious excitement taking place, Mallory dispassionately noted the following in his journal: "The freedmen are holding a protracted meeting near here, largely attended."[9] Given this earlier matter-of-fact observation, it seems that Mallory became concerned only when the freedmen's Christian enthusiasm reached a crescendo in both scope and form that he had never seen before. Therefore, Mallory's words most likely bear witness to a religious transformation among African Americans that began during the war and accelerated with emancipation.

The letters and publications of northern missionary societies working among the freedmen during and after the Civil War support this interpretation. Between 1861 and 1868, organizations such as the American Missionary Association (AMA) and National Freedmen's Relief Association regularly published accounts of religious revivals among African Americans living in Union-occupied areas. The most striking aspect of these reports is that they do not merely describe an awakening of religious enthusiasm among the freedmen but also point to a large number of conversions. In other words, most of the freedmen described were not celebrating their age-old faith but were accepting Christianity for the first time.[10]

The AMA sent ministers and teachers to the Chesapeake region of Virginia and the sea islands of South Carolina shortly after the Union Army occupied those portions of the Confederate coastline in 1861. The AMA annual report for that year indicated that those missions to the freedmen "give some evidence of the presence of the Spirit." In particular, the AMA reported, there had been "the hopeful conversion of several individuals" as well as baptisms for "a number of converts." Significantly, the northern missionaries credited Christian freedmen with improving the conditions for African American conversion. A missionary working in Newport News, Virginia, indicated that "[w]ere it not for the religious element among this people . . . [the freedmen] would be in great despondency." Reverend Lockwood of the Fortress Monroe, Virginia, mission found that the preaching of slave Christian ministers gave their religious meetings tremendous "spirit and power." More important, Lockwood's description of freedmen's sermons reveals the slave Christian core to be actively proselytizing their many unconverted brethren. Free from the obstacles that limited the spread of their faith, the Christian core seized the occasion of emancipation to bring their people to accept Christianity. During a service held near Hampton, Virginia, one slave preacher warned the African American congregation that "I see sinners out of Christ, going to hell." Another admonished his fellow freedmen, "If we would have greater freedom of body, we must first free ourselves from the shackles of sin, and especially the sin of unbelief."[11] Such exhortations were the opening salvos in what would soon be a rapidly expanding and successful battle for the conversion of many unbelieving freedmen.

In the years following 1861, the early missionary reports of modest numbers of African American converts quickly gave way to descriptions of widespread conversion among the newly freed slaves. This rising tide of conversions grew along with the Union Army's occupation of more and more territory both on the periphery of and within the Confederacy. As runaway slaves entered the "contraband camps" and freedmen's settlements that sprung up around the Union Army, white and black Christians greeted them and vigorously sought their conversion. These efforts soon bore much fruit.[12] For example, in 1862, South Carolina missionary Charlotte Forten reported that ministers baptized 150 former slaves on a single Sunday.[13] Reverend Green of Norfolk, Virginia, noted that his Sabbath congregations grew from less than seventy-five to over one thousand participants within three weeks.[14] Missionaries in the contraband camp at Cairo, Illinois, reported that "[d]uring the winter of 1862 there was an almost continuous revival" with conversions occurring "frequently."[15] A year later, North Carolina missionaries exclaimed that "[t]he Lord is doing a great work here . . . and many are being converted to God."[16] Likewise, missionaries from Natchez, Mississippi; Norfolk, Virginia; and St. Louis, Missouri, described conversions at their mission stations as being either "frequent" or "many."[17] Reverend A. D. Olds provided more specific data to describe his successful efforts in the Corinth, Mississippi, contraband camp. Olds reported to the AMA that he had founded the Union Christian Church in the camp with one hundred original covenant signers. He goes on to report that by June 7, 1863, between two and three thousand freedmen attended his church services. Olds found the freedmen's willingness and desire to convert encouraging. Speaking generally about the freedmen's spiritual condition, Olds wrote, "I have been greatly cheered to see with what frankness they confess their sinfulness & their need of a savior."[18] Another Mississippi missionary described conversions among the freedmen as "a deep, quiet work of grace . . . extending almost over the entire colored population."[19] These enthusiastic reports suggest that the pure air of freedom allowed the flame of Christianity to burn brighter than ever before and in doing so forever changed the African American religious landscape.

The diary and letters of Sarah Jane Foster, a missionary teacher among the freedmen of Martinsburg, West Virginia, illustrate just such a spiritual transformation of one African American community. In a letter dated January 14, 1866, Foster noted the "dawning of a religious interest among the [freedmen]." However, while Foster believed she had never attended better prayer meetings than those in Martinsburg, she also indicated that worshipers were "few." Approximately two weeks later, attendance began to increase dramatically. On February 1, 1866, Foster wrote, "I have just returned from a good prayer meeting. . . . Nine or ten manifest a good religious interest. . . . I [also] see great progress in many of my scholars, and the vicious seem to be becoming tractable. Some of the most troublesome are now seeking Christ." By February 11, 1866, Foster reported that the prayer meetings were so full that many had to be turned away. Foster attributed this religious awakening to "a deep and widely spread interest . . . [with] a number . . . seeking to find the Savior." As of March 5, 1866, Foster wrote that "[t]he religious interest yet continues, and there is best evidence of genuine heart work." Finally, on June 18, 1866, Foster declared, "A deep, calm, wide-spread interest still pervades the hearts of the young . . . and has hardly flagged at all since its first awakening nearly six months ago."[20]

Although impressive in its duration, Martinsburg's widespread and sustained religious awakening was not unique. In January 1866, the Methodist newspaper the *Christian Advocate* reported the presence of "several revivals of religion in the Virginia Methodist Churches." According to the newspaper account, the Norfolk district, an AMA mission station since 1862, had experienced "'nearly five hundred conversions' within the last three months." In fact, in its *Twentieth Annual Report* the AMA wrote, "The religious history of the year among the colored people of Eastern Virginia is marked by a great revival." Many others also reported this as a period of tremendous revival in their communities. In Alabama, Bishop M. F. Jamison reported that in 1866,

"I witnessed a powerful awakening, religiously speaking. It capped the climax of all I had ever seen." Mary McCray's family remembered that between November 1866 and June 1867 the free black and freedman community in their Ohio neighborhood witnessed "the greatest revival ever held in that part of the state." The South Carolina Conference of the African Methodist Episcopal Church (AME) described its work as "truly one of the marvels of the age." Following the arrival of two AME missionaries in May 1865, the church's membership exploded from three thousand to above fifty thousand in the span of less than two years.[21]

Another sign of great religious change within the Civil War–era slave and freedmen community was the fact that even males converted in large numbers during this time. Religious revivals were a common occurrence in both the Union and Confederate armies.[22] Scholars estimate that between 100,000 and 200,000 Union soldiers converted during these revivals and countless others participated in the associated services. The unique perspective of African Americans concerning the war made them especially receptive to these periodic revivals. African American soldiers serving with William Tecumseh Sherman marked the occasion of Charleston's surrender with enthusiastic camp meeting revivals. As previously mentioned, Union soldier Zenas T. Haines recalled hearing large numbers of African American soldiers seeking conversion while camped in New Bern, North Carolina. Thomas Johnson declared that "there was one of three things the negro soldier could be found doing when at leisure—'discussing religion,' 'cleaning his musket and accoutrements,' or 'trying to read.'" Elijah Marrs noted that as his unit of the Union Army prepared to go to the front, "some of the new recruits proposed that we have a prayer meeting and preaching in the barracks." That night, after a powerful sermon "set the camp on fire . . . [s]trong men, who had never before been known to bow, fell on their knees for prayer. . . . The next night many professed Christ."[23]

Chaplains in the Union Army described experiencing fruitful revivals among the African American units under their care. Likewise, Thomas Wentworth Higginson's account of army life during the Civil War describes large prayer meetings that attracted both "the warlike and the pious." So many of the freedmen soldiers in Higginson's camp began to attend prayer meetings that at least one Christian freedman complained of this new development. Higginson wrote that Old Jim Cushman "used to vex his righteous soul over the admission of the unregenerate to prayer-meetings, and went off once shaking his head and muttering, 'Too much goat shout wid de sheep.'"[24] Apparently, the wave of African Americans seeking conversion during the Civil War was too much, too soon for Cushman to accept. Having spent his life as one of the Christian core's small band of believers, Cushman probably found the rapid wartime expansion of the faith to be overly convenient in its timing and indiscriminate in its reach.

Mississippi missionaries were among those who witnessed African American men converting during the war. One missionary working among an African American regiment noted, "A glorious revival has begun in connection with our labors here. . . . Fifteen of our soldiers dropped on their knees for prayers, at the moment an opportunity was given."[25] At Fortress Monroe, Virginia, an AMA teacher reported that "[a] great many old men and women are seeking the Savior. . . . Last Sabbath 94 were baptized, a large proportion of them men."[26] Finally, Reverend Edward Ball of Beaufort, North Carolina, recalled that boys led his mission into a deeply spiritual revival. According to Ball, in 1870 "the most powerful revival . . . since the war . . . commenced among the boys in our prayer-meeting, and has extended among the colored people."[27]

There are several reasons for the large number of African American converts to Christianity during and after the Civil War. This momentous change in African American religious life occurred primarily because of the Christian core's faithfulness to Christianity and its accurate prediction of emancipation. For several generations, nonbelieving slaves bore witness to the Christian core's steadfast faith. Despite continuing bondage and, at times, brutal religious persecution, slave Christians clung to their God in anticipation of freedom and eternal life. With their religious prophecy fulfilled, what greater testimony to the power of their God could slave Christians offer prospective converts? Most former slaves accepted the Christian core's interpretation of God as their agent of deliverance. Accordingly, more African Americans than ever before embraced Christianity as their religion in gratitude for all that its God had done for them.

A second reason for the largest period of African American conversion to Christianity was that whites did not control the postbellum church. As Katherine Dvorak demonstrates, most freedmen seized the occasion of emancipation to create their own separate churches. This development received considerable aid from northern African American denominations like the AME Church, already mentioned, and the African Methodist Episcopal Zion Church (AME Zion). As noted by historian William Montgomery, "The bond of race and experience united the [AME and AME Zion] missionaries with the freedmen in ways that whites could never be." Beginning in 1862, this unique bond allowed these denominations to spread their ministry all the way from the contraband camps in the East to Texas in four short years. Because of such efforts and the freedmen's desire for religious independence, by 1871 most African American Christians worshiped in black-majority churches led by black ministers. With this break from the antebellum biracial churches, the masters' message of social control disappeared in favor of the liberating theology celebrated by slave Christians. Gone, too, was the church's endorsement of slavery as a divine institution. Understandably, this new emphasis increased the attractiveness of the faith for African Americans. Daniel Stowell argues that "[a]s black members left the biracial churches and denominations behind, southern black Protestantism experienced a general revival. The freedom and hope born of emancipation led many freedpeople into the newly forming black churches." Joe Gray Taylor seconds Stowell's analysis: "The Negro church finished the Christian evangelism which had begun during slavery times. . . . The mushrooming growth of black churches in the last third of the nineteenth century is evidence enough of their successful missionary endeavor." The movement into separate white and black churches strengthened these attractive properties by providing African Americans with moral and institutional control over a traditionally powerful symbolic presence in the South. The church became the center of the African American community because whites could not destroy or deny legitimacy to a societal institution that they themselves endorsed. In this way, African Americans effectively seized the opportunity to turn the old white-sanctioned institution of control into a vehicle for protection and social change.[28]

A final reason for the widespread conversion of African Americans during the Civil War era was that freedom empowered them to be more effective practitioners of the Christian faith. Beginning with the contraband camps, untold thousands of freedmen gained literacy as a result of the war. Christian missionaries accomplished much of this instruction in literacy. More often than not, teachers combined literacy training and Christian instruction. For example, the AMA openly acknowledged that "[i]n the prosecution of its work among the Freedmen, . . . [i]t commissions no teachers that are not members of some evangelical church, and in all its work endeavors to win men to Christ."[29] An example of such a class was taught by G. W. Carruthers in the Corinth, Mississippi, contraband camp. Carruthers opened his class by having his pupils read scripture "in concert" and then having them repeat it aloud. After Carruthers commented on the text read, he prayed aloud and then had the class recite the Lord's Prayer in unison. Finally, the class sang hymns before breaking into smaller groups for academic instruction.[30] Such instruction effectively turned mission stations like the contraband camps into conversion camps. Not only did this instruction combine with emancipation to bring many African Americans to accept Christianity, but it prepared them to take the faith back into their communities. Armed with literacy, a greater understanding of Christianity, and in many cases their own copy of the Bible, African American Christians of the postbellum era were a formidable force for conversion.[31] For the first time in their history, African American Christians had tangible proof of their God's power, their own churches, freedom of choice to attend services, open access to the Bible, and uncensored preaching. The results of these developments would be staggering.

According to Mechal Sobel, approximately 14.3 percent of the antebellum African American population, north and south, were members of a Christian church. By the late nineteenth century, 32.5 percent, or 2.7 million out of an African American population of 8.3 million, were church members. Thus African American church membership more than doubled within roughly thirty years. While some of this growth reflects the merging of the slaves' invisible institution with formal, public churches, much of it is the result of postbellum conversions. Records indicate that missionaries working among the slaves had far less success in converting African Americans to Christianity than those that came after the Civil War. In 1860, the Southern Baptist Domestic and Indian Mission Board reported that it served 114 churches and baptized 215 African Americans for that year. In contrast, the General Missionary Baptist Association of Tennessee, composed of African American churches, reported in 1869 that it represented 152 churches and baptized 1,456 new members the previous year.[32] In other words, in only its second year of existence, a Tennessee association of freedmen's churches had nearly seven times the number of converts than that of antebellum Southern Baptist missionaries. While the General Missionary Baptist Association of Tennessee did represent 25 percent more churches than the Southern Baptist missionaries, the difference in success is still considerable.

This difference between antebellum and postbellum missionary success would fuel the growth of African American church membership in Georgia, where between 1860 and 1877 the number of black Methodists more than doubled (30,912 to 75,803) and that of black Baptists more than tripled (26,192 to 91,868). Reverend Henry M. Turner of the AME Church described 1866 as a year of revivals in Georgia. In a two-month period, Turner and his subordinates received eleven thousand new members into the AME Church. Turner, as well as other AME missionaries working in the South, reported that "[p]eople who were formerly thought immovable had been brought into the church and 'powerfully converted.'" Likewise, in 1870 the Louisiana Baptist Convention reported that "the increase among the colored people has been remarkable. At the close of the war their membership did not exceed 3,000 now their churches are scattered everywhere throughout the state." Between 1865 and 1871 the number of African American Baptists in Louisiana grew from approximately 3,000 to 30,800 members, leading the state's Baptist Convention to declare this growth as "unparalleled in the history of religious movements." The First and Fourth African Baptist Churches of New Orleans alone baptized nearly three thousand new members between 1866 and 1870. The Bethel Baptist Institutional Church of Jacksonville, Florida, grew to approximately one hundred members during their twenty-seven years of existence before emancipation. In contrast, the church's membership swelled to 1,200 during the twenty-five years after the coming of freedom.[33] A survey of South Carolina African American Baptist churches founded during the

1860s demonstrates a similar pattern of membership growth, particularly through the baptism of new converts. As shown in table 11, total membership for these churches grew from 4,789 to 9,128 between the years 1867 and 1877—over a 90 percent increase. A total of 4,626 baptisms, or new converts, accounted for the bulk of this growth.[34] Clearly, conversions among the freedmen were the leading factor in postbellum African American church growth.

Edward L. Wheeler and James M. Washington both argue that freedom was "the central theme in the history of the black Baptist movement." This study agrees with their findings but would broaden the interpretation to include the entire African American transition to Christianity. Specifically, slave Christians embraced Christianity in part because of their intense desire for freedom. The coming of freedom brought more African Americans than ever to accept Christianity, in addition to equipping them with the tools necessary for continued expansion of the faith. In his study of Louisiana's African American Baptists, William Hicks argued that once "freedom removed the persecutions and oppressions, new zeal for the faith sprang up and the once smothered flame burst forth and its influence spread." So central

TABLE 11. African American Baptist Church Growth in South Carolina, 1867–77

CHURCH NAME	POST OFFICE OR CITY	YEARS	BAPTISMS	MEMBERSHIP GROWTH
Morris St.	Charleston	1867–1877	1,225	1,000–2,216
Calvary	Charleston	1867–1877	725	761–1,364
Tabernacle	Beaufort	1868–1877	614	941–1,475
Lady's Island	Beaufort	1867–1877	438	400–789
Edisto	Edisto	1867–1877	404	1,000–845
Trinity	Florence	1867–1877	275	50–752
Zion	Allendale	1869–1877	235	200–367
Salem	Charleston	1868–1876	165	105–322
Honey Ford	Graham's Turnout	1868–1876	174	118–250
Miller Swamp	Allendale	1869–1876	136	80–272
Mt. Calvary	Buford's Bridge	1869–1876	123	100–301
Wilson's Creek	Storeville	1868–1877	112	34–175

Source: John Allen Middleton, *Directory and Pre-1900 Historical Survey of South Carolina's Black Baptists* (Columbia, SC: J. A. Middleton, 1992).

was freedom to Christianity that in listing his reasons for gratitude to God, Reverend Barney Stone specifically mentioned his deliverance from slavery before he mentioned salvation. Another slave rejected the Christian promise of salvation if he could not be free in this life or the next. According to the narrative of Beverly Jones, Uncle Silas, an elderly Virginia slave, interrupted a church service to ask the minister, "Is us slaves gonna be free in Heaven?" When the minister attempted to avoid the question by telling Uncle Silas that Jesus gave all Christians eternal salvation, the old slave responded, "Gonna give us freedom 'long wid salvation?" Uncle Silas reportedly remained standing throughout the service in expectation of an answer that did not come. Uncle Silas never attended church again.[35]

Albert J. Raboteau rightly argues that Uncle Silas was not alone in his rejection of Christianity without freedom. According to Raboteau, "Some slaves would not accept belief in a supposedly just God who could will or permit slavery." Former slave Charles Ball indicated as much in his personal narrative when he declared, "I could not pray, for the measure of my woes seemed to be full, and I felt as if there was no mercy in heaven, nor compassion on earth, for a man who was born a slave."[36] Clearly, for many slaves freedom was the *sine qua non* for accepting Christianity. Multitudes could not accept Christianity without the hope of future emancipation or would not convert because the prospect of heavenly deliverance seemed unlikely or was unacceptable compensation for God's having originally allowed slavery.

The difference between the percentage of urban and rural slaves who converted to Christianity helps illustrate the central importance of freedom for conversion.[37] In his autobiography, Frederick Douglass wrote, "A city slave is almost a freeman, compared with a slave on the plantation." Douglass himself benefited from urban life by bribing free children to teach him to read and using the anonymity of the city to escape to freedom.[38] Indeed, urban slaves did enjoy much greater freedom of movement and association than did rural slaves. Cities also provided their slaves access to ideas and institutions that were not readily available in the country.[39] As previously noted, large African American churches were one of the unique benefits of city life that urban slaves enjoyed. Thus, urban slaves lived in a more open environment, had greater access to literacy, and had, within certain limita-

tions, their own churches. Considering the advantages available to urban slaves, antebellum city life, more than any other setting in the Old
South, came closest to resembling the conversion-friendly conditions
that developed during and after the Civil War. As a result, more urban
slaves converted to Christianity than did their rural counterparts.[40]

Obviously, any degree of religious freedom could be an agent of
change. This study suggests that in the case of the Civil War, emancipation released a Christian tidal wave that would have washed away
the dominance of the old conjure faiths and left many of its remnants
submerged. The surge of postbellum Christianity likely caused the
conjure faiths to lose their dominance because, as Martha Colquitt
noted, they were incompatible with the beliefs of the orthodox among
the Christian core as well as with those of their newfound allies from
the North. Northern white and black missionaries, who were reared in
a more staid religious tradition, were horrified by the religious practices and worship services conducted by the former slaves and quickly
set out to change them. John Scott of the AMA found the Christian
core so alien that he even doubted their claims to Christianity. In 1870
Scott wrote, "We are told that these people are naturally very religious.
. . . They have got too much religion, but it is not the religion of Christ."
Scott was reacting to the freedmen clergy: "While his religion seemed
based on the Bible and was called Christian, its 'orthodoxy' was like
no western catechism or the written formula of any known Christian
Church."[41] Scott was far from alone in his concerns about the former
slaves' religious beliefs and practices. South Carolina–born Daniel
Alexander Payne of the AME Church was like many who sought to
bring Afro-Christianity into orthodoxy. Payne returned to the South
during the Civil War, and during his long ministerial service there he
witnessed "bush meetings" where ring shouts were performed by the
people he dubbed "Fist and Heel Worshippers." On one occasion, after
viewing the proceedings for nearly fifteen minutes, Payne made the
leader stop the shout and informed the participants "that it was a heathenish way to worship, disgraceful to themselves, to the race, and to
the Christian name."[42]

Because of what they viewed as the former slaves' irregular practices, religious leaders such as Payne and Scott, the organizations
they represented, and religious reformers north and south, black

and white, began widespread efforts to create a more educated clergy among the freedmen. These efforts meshed with ongoing initiatives to provide the freedmen with educational opportunities and in time yielded countless schools and numerous colleges to serve the needs of former slaves. While most former slaves did not achieve high levels of education, institutions like Shaw, Howard, and Hampton began producing an educated black elite in the South. Evelyn Brooks Higginbotham describes this elite as a "race-conscious vanguard imbued with the class values of Victorian America." For these leaders "[t]here was little doubt in their minds that education stood second only to religion in enabling their survival and salvation in America."[43] Educated and upwardly mobile, these elites feared that the legacies of Africa and slavery would hold them back. Daniel Payne provides an excellent example of these concerns in the history of the AME Church. In condemning the Afro-Christian practices of the past, Payne wrote: "These meetings must always be more damaging physically, morally, and religiously, than beneficial. How needful it is to have an intelligent ministry to teach these people who hold to this ignorant mode of worship, the true method of serving God. . . . The time is at hand when the ministry of the African Methodist Episcopal Church must drive out this heathenish mode of worship or drive out all of the intelligent, refined, and practical Christians who may be in her bosom."[44] Inspired and led by persons like Payne, this vanguard would lead the efforts to drive African-derived practices from the freedmen community in general and Afro-Christianity in particular.

The struggle against the old order would not be brief, easy, or completely successful. For many of the Christian core, to abandon the old ways of worship would be to turn away from the faith that brought them deliverance. African-inspired religious practices like the ring shout were ingrained so deeply in the Christian core's religious life that they could not be eliminated from all congregations. In fact, Africanisms remain a significant aspect of Afro-Christianity today throughout parts of the United States and were even more visible during the decades following emancipation. In 1885, Michael Strieby, writing for the AMA, noted, "The old-time [colored] preachers . . . who hold such a strong sway over the people see in the coming change the waning of their power and naturally resist its coming. The people themselves,

reveling in the happy ecstasy of their enkindled emotions, and hug-
ging their vices which are undisturbed thereby, naturally also repel the
light that chills their enjoyment and rebukes their sins. Their religion
cherishes the old vices inherited from slavery."[45] Six years later AMA
observers would still be shocked to find African American churches
where "[c]onversion is to them a series of visions and trances" and parishioners under the "double endowment of the spirit" throw themselves on the floor "in what seemed like a fit." However, despite such
assessments, religious reformers did make significant headway against
practices they found unorthodox at best. Even in the above-described
worship service, the author took some solace that "about a score of
the members look on in despair."[46] Another noted that religious be-
haviors were changing steadily because of educational and genera-
tional differences. In regard to the old slave religious music that Payne
derisively called "corn-field ditties," the author suggested that "the old
negro music will soon disappear." The writer attributed this to the fact
that "[a]ll the educated negro ministers discourage or forbid the use
of it among their people, and the strange, wild songs, whether religious or not, are coming to be regarded as relics and badges of the old
conditions of slavery and heathenism, and the young men and women
are ashamed to sing them."[47] Even the notorious African American social critic William Hannibal Thomas, who had very little positive to say
about his fellow black Americans, echoed this view: "There is growing
up within the race a new school of religious believers, and the cleavage
between them and the old is impossible to close. The old represents
dreams, shadows, misdirected energy, impeached veracity, ephem-
eral fidelity, deficient judgment, and thorough satisfaction with spe-
cious achievement. The new exacts character, consistency, integrity,
industry, common sense, simplicity, clearness, beneficent service, and
above, all fervent piety in word and deed."[48] The progress perceived by
these observers was in large degree a reflection of the fact that many
of the calls for change emanated from the African American community itself.

According to Paul Harvey, African American leaders in the South
"built bureaucracies of benevolence and conceived of 'intelligent worship' as a means of uplifting and educating their plain-folk constitu-
ents." Booker T. Washington, the architect of Tuskegee, proudly touted

how his institution could contribute to this goal. "Having been forti-
fied at Tuskegee by education of mind, skill of hand, Christian character, ideas of thrift, economy, and push and a spirit of independence,
the student is sent out to become a centre of influence and light in
showing the masses of our people in the Black Belt of the South how
to lift themselves up." But while Washington was proud of the work
his institution accomplished for his community, he saw much that still
needed improving if racial uplift was to occur. In particular, Washington complained that in the South "three-fourths of the Baptist ministers and two-thirds of the Methodists are unfit, either mentally or
morally, or both, to preach the Gospel to any one or to attempt to lead
any one." Continuing, he asserted that "the preaching of the colored
ministry is emotional in the highest degree, and the minister consid-
ers himself successful in proportion as he is able to set the people in
all parts of the congregation to groaning, uttering wild screams, and
jumping, finally going into a trance." To remedy the situation, Washington called for the establishment of "undenominational seminaries"
to educate clergy and make them "a great power for good." W. E. B.
Du Bois agreed with Washington that slavery had left the black church
"a great social institution" but one with "ethical ideas warped and
changed and perverted by the whole history of the past; with memories, traditions, and rites of heathen worship, of intense emotion-
alism, trance, and weird singing." To erase the past that he believed
tempted African American ministers and doctors "toward quackery
and demagogy," Du Bois joined Washington in arguing, "The training
of the schools we need to-day more than ever,—the training of deft
hands, quick eyes and ears, and above all the broader, deeper, higher
culture of gifted minds and pure hearts."[49]

For the educated vanguard and its leaders, the pursuit of higher
culture did not include retaining the slaves' spirit-filled worldview
and faith in conjure. Educated blacks feared that as long as these elements of the slave society lingered, African Americans would continue
to find success and equality elusive. They could hardly have ignored
the fascination that whites expressed in regard to the continued presence of "superstition" within the African American community. The
popular press fed this curiosity by offering their readership a steady
diet of stories illustrating in striking language the persistence of the

slaves' old ways. George Washington Cable's description of Voodoo in Louisiana is an excellent example of how many whites viewed or were introduced to these aspects of the older slave world. Of Voodoo Cable wrote, "That worship was as dark and horrid as bestialized savagery could make the adoration of serpents." Such articles and their imagery painted African Americans as immune to reason and incapable of embracing civilization despite being freed. Such perceptions would be harnessed by those eager to deny African Americans their civil liberties at a time when the nation was already beginning to reexamine aspects of Reconstruction policy. For example, the March 1879 issue of the *North American Review* published a series of essays that addressed the questions "Ought the Negro to be Disenfranchised? Ought He to have been Enfranchised?" Such words were met with concern by the educated vanguard as they fully understood what such perceptions and questions could mean for their community. These prospects would motivate these leaders in their efforts against the old order, but they would face the substantial challenge of the continued rural isolation and poverty of much of the African American population. These conditions would allow conjure and its adherents to live on far into the future.[50] However, these leaders were not without advantages and success in this struggle.

While the poverty of the black community and the hated restrictions of Jim Crow aided in the survival of conjure beliefs, those beliefs did not retain their considerable antebellum African American following. Leaders like Booker T. Washington and W. E. B. Du Bois who opposed these religious systems were commanding presences, and their words carried great weight among their race. Education, literacy, and access to modern medicine also whittled away at the former slaves' belief in the old spiritual world and conjure. Succeeding generations would be even more skeptical of their legitimacy. In 1878 students at Hampton University contributed letters describing conjure and its believers to the editors of the *Southern Workman*. The letters published in this series described conjure as overwhelmingly a negative feature of African American life, with at least one author declaring it to be "a curse to their race." This resistance among the young elite was reinforced by white society's attempts to regulate "superstition" out of existence. In 1889 Charles Dudley Warner noted that practitioners of

Voodoo in New Orleans had to move their rituals indoors as all the "semi-public performances have been suppressed." Likewise, in the same era the *New York Times* routinely published articles about conjurers and Voodoo practitioners (often carelessly lumping the two together) who were being prosecuted for medical malpractice, attacked by their own communities, or even declared insane. At the same time, the educated African American vanguard was reinforcing the Christian core's effort to steer the community toward Christianity and away from African religious traditions. All of these factors significantly diminished belief in these once-prominent faiths and slowly but steadily drove them into the shadows as shameful markers of the past or poverty. As a result of this sea change, by 1901 Du Bois could boldly and accurately write, "The Negro church of today is the social centre of Negro life in the United States."[51]

Slaves in antebellum America lived in a world enveloped in darkness. Within the dark night of bondage, a flame of religious hope nurtured by a core of African American Christians offered the promise of light and guidance for those who were attracted to its glow. This flame burned steadily despite the winds of oppression that often caused it to flicker but never extinguished it. Despite its many attractive properties, however, this Christian flame proved too distant to draw all to its warmth; some, wary of its source, stayed far away for fear of being burned. After emancipation, no longer buffeted by the storms of slavery, the flame burned brighter than ever, attracting many to its light in a wave of conversions unprecedented in the history of African Americans. Freedom also allowed those who had long benefited from the flame—the Christian core—to lead others to its healing warmth and form independent churches that served the needs of African Americans first and foremost. In this way, Christianity emerged from slavery and the Civil War to become the dominant faith among African Americans.

CONCLUSION

Throughout this book I have attempted to offer historians another way to interpret the religious lives of antebellum African American slaves. I have drawn upon familiar sources in new ways in order to test existing interpretations and, I hope, expand our understanding of slave religion. I hope that the issues on which I speculate here will prove to be grounds for investigating anew the relationship between African American slaves and Christianity, especially at the state and local levels. The ideas I am most interested in putting forward for examination are, first, that the religious life of African American slaves in the United States was not as dominated by Christianity as scholars have traditionally maintained and, second, that emancipation provided African Americans the greatest incentive to convert. We have underestimated significantly the role of non-Christians within the slave community, as unbelief and several faiths in addition to Christianity were evident among the slaves prior to emancipation. While Afro-Christianity was a significant force within the slave community, I would encourage others to consider the possibility that it was second in importance to New World versions of African Traditional Religions, as reflected in the slaves' spirit-filled worldview and practice of conjure. As suggested in chapter 1, the presence of these different belief systems created visible divisions within the slave population. For example, Muslim slaves might express disdain for the "Christian dogs," while Christian slaves avoided the dances of the "sinners."[1] However, it is unlikely that the slaves' religious differences would have ripped their pluralistic community apart.[2] After all, they shared the experience of enslavement at the hands of a common oppressor. Just as political rivals come together for the good of a nation during wartime, the slaves would have protected one another for the good of the whole. Slavery created conditions that required Voodooists, Christians, and nonreligionists to live side by side peaceably because they needed one another. Ironically, emancipation quickly destroyed what slavery had allowed to survive. With the dawning of a new day of freedom, a tidal wave of Christian conversions eroded the foundation of this thriving religious pluralism. No longer were African Americans "long on religion and short on Christianity."

NOTES

INTRODUCTION

1. Montgomery, *Under Their Own Vine and Fig Tree,* 286.

2. Austin, *African Muslims in Antebellum America: Transatlantic Stories and Spiritual Struggles,* and *African Muslims in Antebellum America: A Sourcebook;* Gomez, *Exchanging Our Country Marks,* and "Muslims in Early America," 671–710; Diouf, *Servants of Allah;* Joseph M. Murphy, *Working the Spirit;* Pinn, *Varieties of African American Religious Experience;* Chireau, *Black Magic: Religion and the African American Conjuring Tradition.*

3. Raboteau, *Slave Religion;* Sobel, *Trabelin' On;* Creel, *A Peculiar People.*

4. Raboteau, *Slave Religion,* 5–16; Sobel, *Trabelin' On,* 122–23. See also Mbiti, *African Religions and Philosophy;* Parrinder, *African Traditional Religion.*

5. Sobel, *Trabelin' On,* 123.

6. Genovese, *Roll, Jordan, Roll;* Blassingame, *The Slave Community;* Levine, *Black Culture and Black Consciousness;* Boles, *Black Southerners,* and *Masters & Slaves in the House of the Lord.*

7. Blassingame, *The Slave Community,* 147.

8. Genovese, *Roll, Jordan, Roll,* 238.

9. Sobel, *Trabelin' On;* Gomez, *Exchanging Our Country Marks;* Stuckey, *Slave Culture: Nationalist Theory and the Foundations of Black America.*

1. AFRO-CHRISTIANITY BY THE NUMBERS

1. Sobel, *Trabelin' On;* Raboteau, *Slave Religion.* Eugene Genovese also argues that "the mass of the slaves apparently became Christians during the late eighteenth and early nineteenth centuries" (Genovese, *Roll, Jordan, Roll,* 184). Sobel, *Trabelin' On,* 182. Some studies even show lower church membership percentages for southerners of all races. For instance, James Daryl Black's study of Baptists in eight Georgia counties shows that only 10 percent of the total white and black population belonged to a Baptist church by 1860. As Baptists were one of the two largest denominations in the South, these figures do not suggest that a majority of whites, much less slaves, were active Christians in the antebellum period (Black, "Contours of Faith," 133).

2. Larry G. Murphy, "Religion in the African-American Community," xxxi–xxxv (see also Pinn, *Varieties of African American Religious Experience,* 1); Gomez, "Muslims in Early America," 671–710; Diouf, *Servants of Allah;* Willis, "From the Dictates of Pride,"

37–55; Kolchin, *American Slavery*, 146 (see also Gomez, *Exchanging Our Country Marks*, 260; Stuckey, *Slave Culture*; Myrdal, *An American Dilemma*, 860; William Johnson, "A Delusive Clothing," 295–311; Sernett, *Black Religion and American Evangelicalism*, 57; Alho, *The Religion of the Slaves*, 189–91).

3. Nichols, *Forty Years of American Life*, 2:263; Olmsted, *The Cotton Kingdom*, 467; James Thomas, *From Tennessee Slave to St. Louis Entrepreneur*, 63.

4. Jones, *The Experience of Thomas H. Jones*, 28.

5. Hughes, *Thirty Years a Slave: From Bondage to Freedom*, 54; Thomas Johnson, *Twenty-Eight Years a Slave in Virginia*, 9.

6. Kemble, *Journal of a Residence on a Georgian Plantation*, 106.

7. Seabury, *The Diary of Caroline Seabury*, 77–78; Parker, *Recollections of Slavery Times*, 67; W. H. Robinson, *From Log Cabin to the Pulpit*, 78; Bibb, *Narrative of the Life and Adventures of Henry Bibb*, 23; Elizabeth, *Elizabeth, A Colored Minister of the Gospel*, 7; Jamison, *Autobiography and Work of Bishop M. F. Jamison*, 47.

8. Randolph, *Sketches of Slave Life*, 14, 30; Thompson, *The Life of John Thompson, A Fugitive Slave*, 85.

9. Friday Jones, *Days of Bondage*, 1; McCray, *Life of Mary F. McCray*, 8–16; Smith, *Autobiography of James L. Smith*, 14; Marrs, *Life and History of the Rev. Elijah P. Marrs*, 32, 68; Williams, *Narrative of James Williams*, 70. Albert J. Raboteau also identifies the division between Christian and "nonreligious" slaves. However, although he describes this segment of the slave population by using the word "many," he limited his coverage of the topic to less than a page (Raboteau, *Slave Religion*, 225).

10. The vast majority of the sources used for the survey are from George Rawick, *American Slave*, vols. 2–19; Supp. Series 1, vols. 1–12; Supp. Series 2, vols. 1–10; and Drew, *A North-Side View of Slavery*; Blassingame, *Slave Testimony*. Slave Narratives are available in the Documenting the American South Collection, University of North Carolina at Chapel Hill, http://docsouth.unc.edu/browse/collections.html.

11. Sobel, *Trabelin' On*, 301.

12. Rawick, *American Slave*, Series 1, South Carolina, 2:26 (William Ballard).

13. The ever-strict Puritans accepted child conversions under the age of nine (Morgan, *The Puritan Family*, 174).

14. Harrison, *The Gospel among the Slaves*, 391. Also, the Ebenezer Baptist Church received Martin Luther King Jr. into church membership at the age of five (Carson, *The Papers of Martin Luther King, Jr.*, 1:361).

15. Loveland, *Southern Evangelicals*, 5.

16. C. W. Miller, "Baptism and Church Membership of Children," 269.

17. Blassingame, *Slave Testimony*, 382.

18. Pollock, *Forgotten Children*, 38.

19. Parsons and Bales, *Family Socialization*, 17. See also Garbarino et al., *Children and Families*, 191; Pollock, *Forgotten Children*, 38–39; Berndt, *Child Development*, 429.

20. Garbarino et al., *Children and Families*, 17.

21. Yinger, *Religion, Society, and the Individual*, 92; Morgan, *The Puritan Family*, 179, 182; Greven, *The Protestant Temperament*, 16; Loveland, *Southern Evangelicals*, 4.

22. Williams, *Aunt Sally, or the Cross the Way of Freedom*, 23. For parents' role in religious training, see also Schwartz, *Born in Bondage*, 121–23; King, *Stolen Childhood*, 67–90.

23. Unless otherwise stated, percentages for all calculations will reflect the proportion of categories for which information is known. For example, the percentages for Upper South and Lower South slaves in the survey reflect the total number of slaves who were born and lived in those regions divided by the total number of the slaves in the survey minus the slaves from unknown origins (i.e., Upper South, 118/345, or 34.2 percent).

24. Kolchin, *American Slavery*, 242.

25. Regional conversion percentages were calculated in the following manner. Adjusted regional births are divided by the number of regional converts. Adjusted regional births are equal to the number of regional births plus or minus the following categories of slaves: minus converted slaves born in a specific region (i.e., Upper or Lower South) without a known location for conversion, minus half of all slaves that converted after moving away to another region, minus half of all unconverted slaves that moved away to another region, plus half of all slaves that moved in from another region. This manner of calculating the regional conversion percentage recognizes the realities of internal migration and the interstate slave trade that saw many Upper South and eastern slaves move farther south and west. In particular, this manner of calculation attempts to share the burden for conversion when an individual lived in both regions being compared.

26. For these calculations East Coast states include Georgia, Maryland, North Carolina, South Carolina, Virginia, and the District of Columbia, while Alabama, Arkansas, Florida, Kentucky, Louisiana, Missouri, Mississippi, Oklahoma, Tennessee, and Texas comprise the southern and western slave states.

27. The ages for the 22 age-specific conversion experiences are as follow: Males (7, 10, 10, 12, 13, 17, 17, 18, 19, 19, 21, 22), Females (9, 10, 10, 10, 12, 13, 15, 15, 17), Unknown Sex (12).

28. It was impossible to identify the region of 13 slaves appearing in earlier occupational data; therefore, these figures represent 111 of the 124 converts with a known occupation.

29. Both John B. Boles and David T. Bailey also argue that independent worship services were not the most common form of slave Christian worship. However, Bailey's figures for slave participation in independent worship services are considerably higher than the findings of this survey. Bailey's study of slave religious services shows that 36 percent of (40) autobiographies and 24 percent of (637) interviews indicate that the author/interviewee attended independent prayer meetings. See Boles, *Masters & Slaves in the House of the Lord*, 10–11; Bailey, "A Divided Prism," 392.

30. Grandy, *Narrative of the Life of Moses Grandy*, 35; Blassingame, *Slave Testimony*, 267 (Charity Bower).

31. Phillips, *American Negro Slavery*; Elkins, *Slavery*.

32. Myers, *The Children of Pride*, 230 (resistance to conversion was not limited to slaves, either. The Reverend and Mrs. C. C. Jones wrote several letters imploring their grown son to seek salvation [see ibid., 120, 348–49]); Rawick, *American Slave*, Series 2, Georgia, pts. 1 &2, 12:46 (Alice Green), Series 2, Georgia. pts. 3 & 4, 13:65 (Ed McCree), Supp. Series 1, Mississippi, pt. 4, 9:1900 (Joe Rollins), and Series 2, Georgia, pts. 3 & 4, 13:329 (Paul Smith). See also Williams, *Narrative of James Williams*, 70–71; Rawick, *American Slave*, Supp. Series 2, Texas, pt. 2, 3:576 (William Byrd); Clayton, *Mother Wit*, 62 (Martin Dragney).

33. Perdue et al., *Weevils in the Wheat,* 100–103 (Cornelius Gardner); Rawick, *American Slave,* Series 2, Georgia, pts. 3 & 4, 13:168 (Uncle Willis), and Series 2, Florida, 17:244 (Louis Napoleon; see also Rawick, *American Slave,* Supp. Series 2, Texas, pt. 7, 8:3040–41 [Ellen Payne]; Swint, *Dear Ones at Home,* 35 [Letter from Lucy Chase to Family, January 29, 1863]; Gannett, "The Freedmen at Port Royal," 10; Alho, *The Religion of the Slaves,* 190); Robinson, *From Log Cabin to the Pulpit,* 24 (W. H. Robinson; see also Rawick, *American Slave,* Supp. Series 2, Texas, pt. 1, 2:393 [Gus Bradshaw]); Douglass, *Narrative of the Life of Frederick Douglas,* 114, 116.

34. Levine, *Black Culture and Black Consciousness;* Abrahams, *Singing the Master.*

35. Rawick, *American Slave,* Series 2, Arkansas, pts. 1 & 2, 8:16 (Marie Clements), Series 1, South Carolina, vol. 3, pts. 3 & 4, 143 (George McAlilley), and Series 1, South Carolina, pts. 3 & 4, 3:105 (Hector Smith; see also Rawick, *American Slave,* Supp. Series 2, Texas, pt. 9, 10:4257 [Willis Winn]), Series 1, Alabama and Indiana, 6:200 (Joseph Holmes), Series 1, Alabama and Indiana, 40 (Siney Bonner; and see also Saxon, Dreyer, and Tallant, *Gumbo Ya-Ya,* 240–41[Charity Parker]; Rawick, *American Slave,* Supp. Series 1, Mississippi, pt. 1, 6:73 [Jim Archer], and Series 2, Fisk Narratives, 18:25 [White Folks Pet]; Genovese, *Roll, Jordan, Roll,* 233).

36. Seabury, *The Diary of Caroline Seabury,* 77–78; Stowe, "Our Florida Plantation," *Atlantic Monthly* 43, 259 (May 1879): 648; See also Stroyer, *My Life in the South,* 45. South Carolina slave Jacob Stroyer noted that some masters found it amusing to force Christian slaves to dance. Stroyer's remembrance that they were forced to dance shows that both whites and blacks recognized a division in the slave community based on the adherence to Christian behavioral standards of the time. It also shows that Christian slaves at least tried to behave differently than other slaves.

37. U.S. Bureau of the Census, *1860 United States Census* (Washington, DC, 1860; out of 393,975 total slave owners, 283,087 owned 1–9 slaves; i.e., 71.85 percent); Genovese, *Roll, Jordan, Roll,* 7.

38. Rawick, *American Slave,* Series 2, Florida, 17:244 (Louis Napoleon; see also Rawick, *American Slave,* Series 2, Arkansas, 8:32–39 [Lucretia Alexander], Series 2, Georgia, 13:281–82 [Georgia Smith], and Series 2, Kansas et al., 16:31–32 [Silas Jackson]; Perdue, *Weevils in the Wheat,* 52, 79 [Archie Booker, Charles Crawley]). Even masters that promoted religious instruction noted that on most plantations the Christians could usually fit inside one cabin. "Where there are pious negroes on a plantation who are so disposed, they should be allowed and encouraged to hold prayer-meetings among themselves; and where the number is too great to be accommodated in one of the negro houses, they should have a separate building for the purposes of worship" (Breeden, *Advice among Masters,* 227).

39. Kolchin, *American Slavery,* 114.

40. Albert, *The House of Bondage,* 23 (Charlotte Brooks). Harriett Gresham described slave prayer meetings as being small in size, "[b]ut the slaves held secret meetings and had praying grounds where they met a few at a time to pray for better things" (Rawick, *American Slave,* Series 2, Florida, 17:159 [Harriett Gresham]).

41. Rawick, *American Slave,* Series 2, North Carolina, 15:373 (Ophelia Whitney), and Series 2, Kansas et al., 75 (William Nelson); Drew, *A North-Side View of Slavery,* 74 (Henry Banks; see also page 97 [James Sumler]; Rawick, *American Slave,* Series 2, North

Carolina, 15:314 [Annie Stephenson], and Series 1, Alabama and Indiana, 6:173 [Charity Grigsby]).

42. "Destitution of Religious Knowledge," *Alabama Baptist Advocate,* March 20, 1850, 2.

43. "Address of the Bishops," *Journal of the General Conference of the Methodist Episcopal Church, South* (May 1858): 392.

44. "Georgia," *Southern Baptist Missionary Journal* (June 1849): 18.

45. "Report on Domestic Missions," *Minutes of the Twenty-Seventh Anniversary of the Alabama State Convention* (M. D. J. Slade, 1850): 15–17. Typescript from Una Roberts Lawrence Collection, Southern Baptist Historical Library and Archives, Nashville, Tennessee.

46. Willis, "From the Dictates of Pride," 51; Sobel, *Trabelin' On,* 182; Raboteau, *Slave Religion,* 209.

47. Friedman, *The Enclosed Garden,* 4; Frazier, "Religion and Women," 1563; Frey and Wood, *Come Shouting to Zion,* 163. The testimony of former slaves agrees with this interpretation. See Clayton, *Mother Wit,* 104, 148 (Elizabeth Ross Hite, Rosie King).

48. Willis, "From the Dictates of Pride," 37–55.

49. U.S. Bureau of the Census, *1860 United States Census.*

50. "The Religious Training of Children," *The Commission* (October 1856): 103. See also "Pastoral Address of the Fourth General Conference of the Methodist Episcopal Church, South," *Quarterly Review of the Methodist Episcopal Church, South* (July 1858): 425; Owen, *The Sacred Flame of Love,* 41; Sernett, *Black Religion and American Evangelicalism,*71; Bode, "The Formation of Evangelical Communities in Middle Georgia," 722–24.

51. "Sunday Schools for Slaves," *Christian Observer,* May 13, 1848, 77.

52. Randall Miller, *"Dear Master,"* 224.

53. Jones, Phillips, and Glunt, *Florida Plantation Records,* 31.

54. Raboteau, *Slave Religion,* 149.

55. Alabama Baptist Convention, *Minutes of the Thirty-Second Anniversary of the Alabama Baptist State Convention, Held at Montgomery, May 9th and 10th, 1855, and of the Alabama Baptist Bible Society Held at the Same Time and Place* (publisher and date of publication unknown), 2. Typescript from Una Roberts Lawrence Collection, Southern Baptist Historical Library and Archives, Nashville, Tennessee.

56. "Important City Missions," *Home and Foreign Journal* (April 1855): 1.

57. Frey and Wood, *Come Shouting to Zion,* 162.

58. Bailey, "Frontier Religion," 1286–88.

59. Williams, *Narrative of James Williams,* 70. See also Ball, *Fifty Years in Chains,* 142.

60. Albert, *The House of Bondage,* 11 (Charlotte Brooks).

61. Harrison, *The Gospel among the Slaves,* 281.

62. Paxton, *A History of the Baptists of Louisiana,* 121.

63. Genovese, *Roll, Jordan, Roll,* 7–10.

64. U.S. Bureau of the Census, *1860 United States Census.*

65. Harrison, *The Gospel among the Slaves,* 323; Southern Baptist Convention, *Proceedings of the Southern Baptist Convention Eighth Biennial Session . . . Savannah, Ga., May 10th, 11th, 12th and 13th* (Richmond: 1861), 32–34, in Southern Baptist Historical Library and Archives, Nashville, Tennessee.

66. "Religious Instruction of the Negroes," *Quarterly Review of the Methodist Episco-*

pal Church, South (July 1847): 319–38; C. C. Jones, "Suggestions on the Religious Instructions of the Negroes in the Southern States," 1–30.

67. "The Religious Instruction of Slaves," *Biblical Recorder,* February 4, 1853, 1.

68; "The Religious Instruction of the Negroes," *African Repository and Colonial Journal* (December 1844): 381.

69. Raboteau, *Slave Religion,* 196–207. Likewise, of the twenty-eight Southern Baptist church minute books consulted by Mechal Sobel in *Trabelin' On,* six, or nearly one in four, are from urban areas.

70. Boothe, *The Cyclopedia of the Colored Baptists of Alabama,* 240.

2. CHRIST IN CHAINS

1. Charles Joyner, "'Believer I Know,'" in Paul Johnson, *African-American Christianity: Essays in History,* 37. In *American Slavery, 1619–1877,* Peter Kolchin suggested that the reaction to Phillips and Elkins led historians to overstate evidence for the "slaves' resiliency and autonomy" and subsequently he pointed to the need for "modifications" in the interpretation of slave life (Kolchin, *American Slavery,* 137–38); Philip D. Morgan seconds Kolchin's dissent (Morgan, *Slave Counterpoint,* 442–43).

2. See quotes on religious destitution in chap. 1 of this book. Winthrop D. Jordan's study of a Civil War slave conspiracy provides a nice overview of the religious "destitution" that even existed in an established old southwestern cotton county in Mississippi (Jordan, *Tumult and Silence,* 189–95).

3. Southern Baptist Convention, *Proceedings of the Southern Baptist Convention* (Richmond: H. K. Ellyson, 1853): 11, in Southern Baptist Historical Library and Archives, Nashville, Tennessee; Southern Baptist Convention, *Proceedings of the Southern Baptist Convention* (Richmond: H. K. Ellyson, 1859), 11, in Southern Baptist Historical Library and Archives, Nashville, Tennessee.

4. McWhiney, Moore, and Pace, *"Fear God and Walk Humbly,"* 8, 32, 101, 199; Cain, *Methodism in the Mississippi Conference, 1846–1870,* 190; "Report on North and South Santee Mission," *Christian Advocate* 19 (September 1834): 14; Harrison, *The Gospel among the Slaves,* 265–66. See also Sernett, *Black Religion and American Evangelicalism,* 65; White, "The Glory of Southern Christianity," 115.

5. "From Our Missionaries," *Southern Baptist Missionary Journal* (November 1846): 1 (see also Southern Baptist Convention, *Proceedings of the Southern Baptist Convention* [Richmond: 1845]: 33–35, in Southern Baptist Historical Library and Archives, Nashville, Tennessee; "Report on Domestic Missions," *Minutes of the Twenty-Seventh Anniversary of the Alabama State Convention* [M. D. J. Slade, 1850]: 15–17 [typescript from Una Roberts Lawrence Collection, Southern Baptist Historical Library and Archives, Nashville, Tennessee]); Zanca, "Letter from Mother Hyacinth LeConnait to her brother, March 24, 1856," in *American Catholics and Slavery,* 161.

6. "A Call from Texas," *Christian Advocate,* April 3, 1835, 194; Southern Baptist Convention, "Need of Domestic Missionaries," in *Proceedings of the Southern Baptist Convention Eighth Biennial Session* (Richmond, 1861), 57, in Southern Baptist Historical Library and Archives, Nashville, Tennessee; "Demand for Labor," *Southern Baptist Missionary*

Journal (July 1848): 46; "Reformation of the Colored Population," *South-Western Baptist,* March 2, 1854, 2; "Delaware and MD, a Missionary Field," *Christian Observer,* June 20, 1845, 97; "Speech of Rev. Dr. Newton," *Christian Observer,* November 11, 1854, 177–78; "Southern Aid Society," *Christian Observer,* November 25, 1854, 185; Methodist Episcopal Church, South, "Address of the Bishops," in *Journal of the General Conference of the Methodist Episcopal Church, South* (May 1858): 392; "The Domestic Mission Board," *Alabama Baptist* September 12, 1846, 2 (see also Bethel Baptist Association, *Minutes of the Bethel Baptist Association [Kentucky], 1847,* 11, in Southern Baptist Historical Library and Archives, Nashville, Tennessee; Bethel Baptist Association, *Minutes of the Bethel Baptist Association [Alabama], 1850,* 11, in Southern Baptist Historical Library and Archives, Nashville, Tennessee; Harrison, *The Gospel among the Slaves,* 302); "Men and Means Wanted," *Christian Observer,* October 29, 1853, 174; Taylor, *Louisiana Reconstructed,* 440. And see also Zanca, "Letter from Bishop William Elder of Natchez, MS to Propagation of the Faith, 1858," in *American Catholics and Slavery, 236.*

7. William A. Clebsch, "Journal of the Proceedings of an Adjourned Convention of Bishops, Clergymen and Laymen of the Protestant Episcopal Church in the Confederate States of America (1861)," in *Journals of the Protestant Episcopal Church in the Confederate States of America,* pt. 2, 42; "Delaware and MD, a Missionary Field," *Christian Observer,* June 20, 1845, 97; C. C. Jones, *The Religious Instruction of the Negroes,* 98; "[From the Richmond Christian Advocate] Religious Instruction of Negroes," *African Repository and Colonial Journal* (July 1856): 215 (see also Loveland, *Southern Evangelicals,* 230–32); Travis, *Rev. Joseph Travis, A.M., a Member of the Memphis Annual Conference,* 164; Zanca, "Letter from Bishop Bishop Augustin Verot of St. Augustine, Florida to Propagation of the Faith, July 14, 1860," in *American Catholics and Slavery,* 241; "Pon Pon Mission," *Christian Advocate,* January 1, 1845), 82; Harrison, *The Gospel among the Slaves,* 268–69; Baudier, *The Catholic Church in Louisiana,* 433; White, "The Glory of Southern Christianity," 117.

8. Ammerman, *Baptist Battles,* 32; Ownby, *Subduing Satan,* 126–27.

9. Rawick, *American Slave,* Series 2, Kansas et al., 16:22 (Fleming Clark), Series 1, Texas, pts. 1 & 2, 4:122 (Ann Hawthorne), Series 1, South Carolina, pts. 1 & 2, 2:100 (Josephine Bristow), Supp. Series 1, Mississippi, pt. 5, 10:2075 (Hattie Sugg), and Rawick, Series 2, North Carolina, 14:4–5 (Louisa Adams); Pennington, *The Fugitive Blacksmith,* 43; Rawick, *American Slave,* Series 2, Arkansas, pt. 7, and Missouri, 11:53 (Betty Brown; see also page 155 [Columbus Williams], and Supp. Series 1, Mississippi, pt. 5, 10:1938 [Simmons Smith]; Perdue, *Weevils in the Wheat,* 82, 130 [Baily Cunningham, Della Harris]; Clayton, *Mother Wit,* 38, 44, 147 [Henrietta Butler, Manda Cooper, Hannah Kelly]; Sernett, *Black Religion and American Evangelicalism,* 63).

10. For instance, the master of Jane Thompson made her go outside when his family held family prayers. John Bates's master stopped taking his slaves to church with him and confiscated a literate slave's Bible once the slaves connected Christianity to freedom (see also Rawick, *American Slave,* Series 2, Arkansas, pt. 7, and Missouri, 11:353 [Jane Thompson], and Supp. Series 2, Texas, pt. 1, 2:214 [John Bates]; Jordan, *Tumult and Silence,* 193–95). Jones, *The Experience of Thomas H. Jones,* 28 (Thomas Jones); C. C. Jones, *The Religious Instruction of the Negroes,* 117, 184. Reminder: If a slave was permitted to attend church with his master only once a year, then his master was counted as permitting slaves to and providing them with worship.

11. Rawick, *American Slave,* Series 1, Alabama and Indiana, 6:26 (Callie Bracey), ibid., 237 (Emma Jones), Series 2, Kansas et al., 16:40 (David Hall) and Series 2, North Carolina, 14:94 (John Becton).

12. Rawick, *American Slave,* Series 1, South Carolina, pts. 1 & 2, 2:192 (Sylvia Cannon), and Series 1, Alabama and Indiana, 6:295 (Sally Murphy; see also Rawick, *American Slave,* Supp. Series 2, Texas, pt. 9, 10:4279 [Willis Woodsen]), Supp. Series 1, Mississippi, pt. 1, 6:157 (Manda Boggan; see also Rawick, *American Slave,* Series 2, Arkansas, pts. 5 & 6, 10:182 [Tom Neal], Supp. Series 1, Mississippi, pt. 5, 10:2241 [Robert Weathersby]), Series 2, Fisk University Narratives, 19:188 (Sixty-Five Years a Washer and Ironer), Series 2, Kansas et al., 16:32 (Rev. Silas Jackson; also see Series 2, Florida, 17:67 [Charles Coates]).

13. Rawick, *American Slave,* Series 2, Kansas et al., 16:7 (Susan Bledsoe), Series 1, Alabama and Indiana, 6:160 (Ella Grandberry), Series 2, Arkansas, pt. 7, and Missouri, 143 (Lou Griffin), Series 1, Texas, pts. 3 & 4, 5:56 (Isaac Martin), Series 1, Alabama and Indiana, 6:68 (Henry Cheatam); Williams, *Narrative of James Williams,* 71 (James Williams); Rawick, *American Slave,* Series 2, Fisk University Narratives, 18:121 (Joseph Farley), and Series 2, Georgia, pts. 3 & 4, 13:142 (Green Willbanks). See also Randolph, *Slave Cabin to the Pulpit.*

14. Rawick, *American Slave,* Series 2, Arkansas, pts. 1 & 2, 8:117 (Spencer Barnett), Series 2, Florida, 17:199 (Randall Lee), Series 2, Kansas et al., 16:67 (Millie Simpkins); *Born in Slavery: Slave Narratives from the Federal Writers' Project, 1936–38,* Texas Narratives, vol. 16, pt. 2 (Federal Writers' Project, United States Work Progress Administration, Manuscript Division, Library of Congress), 92, http://memory.loc.gov/ammem/ snhtml/snhome.html (O.W. Green); Rawick, *American Slave,* Series 1, Alabama and Indiana, 6:39–40 (Siney Bonner; see also Rawick, *American Slave,* Supp. Series 1, Indiana and Ohio, 5:166 [Nelson Polk]), Series 2, Florida, 17:279 (Anna Scott; see also Perdue, *Weevils in the Wheat,* 71 [Samuel Chilton]; Rawick, *American Slave,* Series 1, Alabama and Indiana, 6:26 [Callie Bracey]); Elkton Baptist Church, "Elkton Baptist Church Minutes, Elkton, Kentucky 1825–1909" (March 1846), in Southern Baptist Historical Library and Archives, Nashville, Tennessee; C. C. Jones, *The Religious Instruction of the Negroes,* 158.

15. Rawick, *American Slave,* Series 1, Alabama and Indiana, 6:416 (Mingo White), and ibid., 162 (Ella Grandberry).

16. For example, Thomas Jones credited secret, independent readings with giving him his first notions about God and inspiring him to seek Christian conversion (Jones, *The Experience of Thomas H. Jones,* 22; see also Blassingame, *Slave Testimony,* 466 [Richard Parker]). "Report on the Instruction of the Colored Population," *Southern Baptist Missionary Journal* (July 1849): 39. Southern Baptists were not alone in this belief (Genovese, *A Consuming Fire,* 23; see also "The Bible among the Slaves," *Christian Observer,* April 15, 1848, 62; "Instruction of Slaves," *African Repository and Colonial Journal* [January 1856]: 16–17; "Report of the Directors of the Society of the United Brethren for Propagating the Gospel among the Heathen," *United Brethren's Missionary Intelligencer and Religious Miscellany* 5, no. 6 [1835]: 245–46); Southern Baptist Convention, "Religious Instruction of the Colored Population," in *Proceedings of the Southern Baptist Convention* (Richmond: Dispatch Steam Press, 1866), 85–86, in Southern Baptist Historical Library and Archives, Nashville, Tennessee. For restrictions on slave literacy, see Geno-

vese, *Roll, Jordan, Roll,* 562; and C. C. Jones, *The Religious Instruction of the Negroes,* 115; Sernett, *Black Religion and American Evangelicalism,* 65.

17. C. C. Jones, *The Religious Instruction of the Negroes,* 157, 563.

18. "Report of the Directors of the Society of the United Brethren for Propagating the Gospel among the Heathen," *United Brethren's Missionary Intelligencer and Religious Miscellany* 5, no. 6 (1835): 245–46; Crabtree and Patton, *"Journal of a Secesh Lady,"* 21 (see also Weiner, *Mistresses and Slaves,* 80–81; Chesnut, *A Diary from Dixie,* 171).

19. Rawick, *American Slave,* Series 2, Arkansas, pt. 7, and Missouri, 11:365–66 (Minksie Walker).

20. "Report on the Instruction of the Colored Population," *Southern Baptist Missionary Journal* (July 1849): 39.

21. Catherine Edmonston described using Dr. Watt's catechism to instruct her slaves (Crabtree and Patton, *"Journal of a Secesh Lady,"* 21). Watts, *Dr. Watt's Plain and Easy* Catechism (see also [Methodist] Capers, *A Catechism for Little Children;* [Baptist] Chambliss, *The Catechetical Instructor;* and [Presbyterian] Charles C. Jones, *Catechism of Scripture, Doctrine, and Practice*).

22. Rawick, *American Slave,* Series 2, Arkansas, pts. 5 & 6, 10:190 (Ervin Smith). See also Perdue, *Weevils in the Wheat,* 241 (Sister Robinson).

23. Rawick, *American Slave,* Series 2, Georgia, pts. 1 & 2, 12:77 (Arie Binns).

24. C. C. Jones, *Religious Instruction of the Negroes,* 21; Clarke, *Wrestlin' Jacob,* 37. See also Genovese, *Roll, Jordan, Roll,* 204–5; Alho, *The Religion of the Slaves,* 164.

25. Matthew 7:13–14.

26. C. C. Jones, *The Religious Instruction of the Negroes,* 117.

27. Elkins, *Slavery,* 81–82.

28. Levine, *Black Culture and Black Consciousness;* Abrahams, *Singing the Master.*

29. Ball, *Fifty Years in Chains,* 15; Perdue, *Weevils in the Wheat,* 181 (Beverly Jones).

30. Wightman, *Life of William Capers,* 296; Genovese, *Roll, Jordan, Roll,* 186–87; Raboteau, *Slave Religion,* 152; White, "The Glory of Southern Christianity," 113; Harrison, *The Gospel among the Slaves,* 150–51; C. C. Jones, "Suggestions on the Religious Instruction of the Negroes in the Southern States," *Princeton Review* (January 1848): 1–30; Wightman, *Life of William Capers,* 295–96.

31. Genovese, *Roll, Jordan, Roll,* 190–92; Raboteau, *Slave Religion,* 152; Creel, *A Peculiar People,* 7; Genovese, *Roll, Jordan, Roll,* 166–67. See also Blassingame, *The Slave Community,* 86.

32. Ball, *Fifty Years in Chains,* 15; Randolph, *Slave Cabin to the Pulpit,* 198; Bibb, *Narrative of the Life and Adventures of Henry Bibb,* 24; Rawick, *American Slave,* Series 2, Arkansas, pts.. 5 & 6, 10:332 (Emma Tidwell), Series 2, Arkansas, pt. 7, and Missouri, 11:303 (Alice Sewell; for evidence of the widespread non-salvation-based messages see also in Rawick, *American Slave,* Series 1, Texas, 5:208–17 [Jenny Proctor], Series 1, Alabama and Indiana, 6:397–400, 158–61 [Charlie Van Dyke, Candus Richardson], Series 2, Florida, 17:54, 139–45, 250–56 [Aunt Bess, Clayborn Gantling, Margaret Nickerson], Supp. Series 1, Mississippi, pt. 5, 10:1978–87, 2358 [Berry Smith, Frances Willis], Supp. Series 1, Oklahoma, 12:78–81 [Robert Burns], and Supp. Series 2, Texas, 2:397–404 [Wes Brady]; Perdue, *Weevils in the Wheat ,* 320 [Nancy Williams]; Rawick, *American Slave,* Series 2, Fisk Narratives, 18:45 [Slaves Have No Souls]), Series 2, Georgia, pts.. 1 & 2, 12:20 (Hannah

Austin); Rawick, *American Slave,* Series 2, Georgia, pts. 3 & 4, 13:201 (Henry Wright; see also Perdue, *Weevils in the Wheat,* 305 [Bacchus White]; Rawick, *American Slave,* Series 2, Fisk Narratives, 18:82 [Massa's Slave Son], Supp. Series 1, Mississippi, pt. 2, 7:373 [Ned Chaney]), Series 2, Georgia, pts. 1 & 2, 12:131 (Tom Hawkins).

33. Rawick, *American Slave,* Series 1, South Carolina, pts. 1 & 2, 3:194–95 (Cureton Milling), Series 2, North Carolina, pt. 2, 15:270 (John Smith), and Series 2, North Carolina, pt. 1, 14:217 (Mattie Curtis); Rawick, *American Slave,* Series 2, Georgia, pts. 1 & 2, 12:12 (Leah Garrett; see also Drew, *A North-Side View of Slavery,* 91, 105–6, 334, 338 [David West, Charles Peyton Lucas, William Humbert, Lydia Adams]; Sernett, *Black Religion and American Evangelicalism,* 86–91); Douglass, *Narrative of the Life of Frederick Douglass,* 153–54.

34. Roper, *A Narrative of the Adventures and Escape of Moses Roper,* 51; Steward, *Twenty-Two Years a Slave,* 98 (Austin Steward); Jacobs, *Incidents in the Life of a Slave Girl,* 403 (her mistress's lack of Christian sympathy also did not impress Harriet Jacobs; see pg. 347); Ball, *Fifty Years in Chains,* 32 (Charles Ball); Albert, *The House of Bondage,* 68–69 (Lorendo Goodwin); Mason, *Life of Isaac Mason as a Slave,* 27.

35. For recent discussions of white and black shared religious experiences, see James, "Biracial Fellowship in Antebellum Baptist Churches," and Hall, "Black and White Christians in Florida, 1822–1861," in Boles, *Masters & Slaves in the House of the Lord,* 37–57, 81–98; Flynt, *Alabama Baptists,* 42–47; Raboteau, *Slave Religion,* 314.

36. Rawick, *American Slave,* Series 1, Alabama and Indiana, 6:417 (Mingo White); Rawick, *American Slave,* Series 1, South Carolina, pts. 1 & 2, 2:152 (C. B. Burton; see also pages 26, 241, 304, 209 [William Ballard, John Davenport, Wallace Davis, Fannie Griffin]), Series 2, Georgia, pts. 1 & 2, 12:52 (Georgia Baker; see also Dennard, "Religion in the Quarters," 83–87; Butler, "The Creation of African American Christianity," 182).

37. Drew, *A North-Side View of Slavery,* 338 (Lydia Adams; see also pages 79, 51, 98–99 [Henry Atkinson, Nancy Howard, James Sumler]; Albert, *The House of Bondage,* 80 [Octavia Rogers]); Bibb, *Narrative of the Life and Adventures of Henry Bibb,* 39 (Henry Bibb); Blassingame, *Slave Testimony,* 411 (Joseph Smith; see also pages 420, 435, 696 [Susan Boggs, Isaac Throgmorton, Lewis Hayden]); Perdue, *Weevils in the Wheat,* 224 (Matilda Perry). Likewise, Harriet Tubman refused to join her master's family in prayer. While her white masters held prayer meeting in their home, Harriet removed herself to the landing and prayed independently (Blassingame, *Slave Testimony,* 458 [Harriet Tubman]). Rawick, *American Slave,* Series 1, Alabama and Indiana, 6:193 (Katie Sutton); American Missionary Association, *Twenty-Second Annual Report of the American Missionary Association* (New York: American Missionary Association, 1868), 36; Alho, *The Religion of the Slaves,* 134.

38. Genovese argues that the slaves understood the failure of hoodoo to work on whites as being the result of natural differences. According to Genovese, "[B]ecause the one had originated in Europe and the other in Africa . . . this difference in origin somehow meant that they were subject to different natural forces" (Genovese, *Roll, Jordan, Roll,* 222). For examples of slave disregard for white Christianity, see Rawick, *American Slave,* Series 2, Florida, 17:97–98 (Douglas Dorsey), and Series 1, South Carolina, pts. 3 & 4, 3:5 (Cordelia Jackson). See also Perdue, *Weevils in the Wheat,* 322 (Nancy Williams).

39. Rawick, *American Slave,* Series 2, Georgia, pts. 1 & 2, 12:258 (Minnie Davis; see

also Genovese, *Roll, Jordan, Roll,* 238); Rawick, *American Slave,* Series 2, Georgia, pts. 1 &
2, 12:329 (Mary Ferguson), Series 1, South Carolina, pts. 1 & 2, 2:163 (Solbert Butler).

40. Rawick, *American Slave,* Supp. Series 1, Mississippi, pt. 3, 8:965 (Wash Hayes; see
also Pennington, *The Fugitive Blacksmith,* 12; Perdue, *Weevils in the Wheat,* 100 [Corne-
lius Gardner]; C. C. Jones, *The Religious Instruction of the Negroes,* 118); Parker, *Recollections of Slavery Times,* 67 (Allen Parker; for Sunday as "Visiting Day," see Rawick, *American Slave,* Series 2, Arkansas, pts. 3 & 4, 9:121 [Lee Guidon], Series 1, South Carolina, pts.
3 & 4, 3:239 [Sallie Paul], Series 2, Georgia, pts.. 1 & 2, 12:248 [Easter Huff]; Brown, *Narrative of William Wells Brown,* 36; Rawick, *American Slave,* Series 1, South Carolina, pts. 1
& 2, 2:2 [M. E. Abrams]. For other Sunday diversions, see Rawick, *American Slave,* Series
2, Kansas et al., 16:22 [Fleming Clark], Series 2, Georgia, pts. 1 & 2, 12:269 [Mose Davis],
Series 1, Alabama and Indiana, 6:107 [Matthew Hume], and Series 2, Arkansas, pt. 7, and
Missouri, 11:267 [Eliza Overton]; Bibb, *Narrative of the Life and Adventures of Henry Bibb,*
23; Stroyer, *My Life in the South,* 50; Rawick, *American Slave,* Series 2, Georgia, pts. 1 & 2,
12:6 [Elisha Garey]. For examples of slaves working for themselves on Sunday, see Rawick, *American Slave,* Series 2, North Carolina, pt. 2, 15:166 [Lily Perry], Series 2, Kansas et
al., 16:29 [Hannah Davidson], and Series 2, Arkansas, pt. 7, and Missouri, 11:40 [George
Bollinger]; Bruce, *The New Man,* 51; Rawick, *American Slave,* Series 1, South Carolina,
pts. 3 & 4, 3:219 [William Oliver]; Baker and Baker, *The WPA Oklahoma Slave Narratives,*
342 [Alice Rawlings]); C. C. Jones, *The Religious Instruction of the Negroes,* 138; Olmsted,
A Journey in the Seaboard Slave States, 113–14.

41. Olmsted, *A Journey in the Seaboard Slave States,* 114; Rawick, *American Slave,* Se-
ries 2, Kansas et al., 16:30 (Hannah Davidson; see also Loguen, *The Rev. J. W. Loguen,* 105;
Genovese, *Roll, Jordan, Roll,* 207; Alho, *The Religion of the Slaves,* 164); Rawick, *American
Slave,* Series 1, South Carolina. pts. 3 & 4, 3:210 (Sena Moore), Series 1, Alabama and
Indiana, 6:107 (Matthew Hume); Brown, *Narrative of William Wells Brown,* 37; Rawick,
American Slave, Supp. Series 1, Georgia, pt. 1, 3:219 (Arthur Colson), and Series 1, Ala-
bama and Indiana, 6:145 (George Morrison); Perdue, *Weevils in the Wheat,* 287 (Horace
Tonsler). See also Rawick, *American Slave,* Series 2, Georgia, pts. 1 & 2, 12:186 (Ellen
Claibourn).

42. Rawick, *American Slave,* Series 2, Kansas et al., 16:14 (Robert Falls), Supp. Series
1, Mississippi, pt. 5, 10:2058 (Isaac Stier; for slaves who emphasized food at worship services, see also Rawick, *American Slave,* Series 2, Georgia, pts. 1 & 2, 12:204 [John Hill],
Series 2, Kansas et al., 16:3–4 [Julia Carey]), Series 1, Texas, pts. 3 & 4, 5:96 [Tom Mills;
for slaves who recalled courting during worship services, see Rawick, *American Slave,*
Series 2, Georgia, pts. 3 & 4, 13:61 [Ed McCree], Series 2, Arkansas, pts. 5 & 6, 182 [Tom
Neal], and Supp. Series 1, Mississippi, pt. 2, 7:384 [Hannah Chapman]; Furman, *Slavery
in the Clover Bottoms,* 46); Rawick, *American Slave,* Series 2, Georgia, pts. 1 & 2, 5–6 (Elisha Garey); Perdue, *Weevils in the Wheat,* 108 (Candis Goodwin).

43. Loguen, *The Rev. J. W. Loguen,* 105. See also Blassingame, *The Slave Community,* 130.

44. Rawick, *American Slave,* Series 2, Georgia, pts. 1 & 2, 12:204 (John Hill), Supp.
Series 2, Texas, pt. 2, 3:576 (William Byrd). See also Rawick, *American Slave,* Supp. Series
1, Indiana and Ohio, 5:68 (Rachel Duncan).

45. Wightman, *Life of William Capers,* 299; "Address of the Bishops to the Fourth
General Conference of the Methodist Episcopal Church, South," *Quarterly Review of the*

Methodist Episcopal Church, South (July 1858): 415; Clebsch, "Journal of the Proceedings of an Adjourned Convention of Bishops, Clergymen and Laymen of the Protestant Episcopal Church in the Confederate States of America (1861)," in *Journals of the Protestant Episcopal Church in the Confederate States of America*, pt. 2, 42; Ten Islands Baptist Association, *Minutes of the Proceedings of the Ten Islands Baptist Association Held at Post Oak Spring, Calhoun County, Alabama, on the 26th, 27th and 28th days of September, 1863* (Alabama?: s.n., 1863), 6, http://docsouth.unc.edu/imls/tenislands/menu.html; C. C. Jones, *Religious Instruction of the Negroes: An Address*, 11, 125.

46. U.S. Bureau of the Census, *1860 United States Census*. The nine black majority counties used for this average are Camden, Dougherty, McIntosh, Glascock, Glynn, Putnam, Burke, Baker, Montgomery.

47. Southern Baptist Convention, *Proceedings of the Southern Baptist Convention Seventh Biennial Session* (Richmond, 1859), 60, in Southern Baptist Historical Library and Archives, Nashville, Tennessee.

48. Bethel Baptist Association, *Minutes of the Bethel Baptist Association (Alabama), 1857*, 11. Typescript in Southern Baptist Historical Library and Archives, Nashville, Tennessee.

49. Alabama Baptist State Convention, *Minutes of the Forty-First Annual Session of the Alabama Baptist State Convention, 1863*, 1. Typescript from Una Roberts Lawrence Collection in Southern Baptist Historical Library and Archives, Nashville, Tennessee.

50. Genovese, *A Consuming Fire*. See also Stowell, *Rebuilding Zion*, 38, 180; Cheesebrough, *"God Ordained This War,"* 238–39; Foster, *History of the Tuscaloosa County Baptist Association*, 87; Boles, *Masters & Slaves in the House of the Lord*, 11; St. Amant, *A Short History of Louisiana Baptists*, 36–37; Baudier, *The Catholic Church in Louisiana*, 433.

3. ALTERNATIVES TO CHRISTIANITY
WITHIN THE ANTEBELLUM SLAVE COMMUNITY

1. Mbiti, *African Religions and Philosophy*, 1–2 (see also Chireau, "Conjure and Christianity in the Nineteenth Century," 225); Coleman, *Tribal Talk*, 31; Jesse Gaston Mulira, "The Case of Voodoo in New Orleans," in Holloway, *Africanisms in American Culture*, 37.

2. Butler, *Awash in a Sea of Faith*, 158; Blassingame, *The Slave Community*, 35.

3. Raboteau, *Slave Religion*, 43–92; Sobel, *Trabelin' On*, 3–75; Genovese, *Roll, Jordan, Roll*, 209–17.

4. Jon Butler describes this process as an "African spiritual holocaust" (Butler, *Awash in a Sea of Faith*, 129–163). Archaeologist Charles E. Orser goes so far as to say such an interpretation is "naive" (Orser, "The Archaeology of African-American Slave Religion in the Antebellum South," 35). Philip D. Morgan also finds Butler's argument for an "African spiritual holocaust" to be less than persuasive (Morgan, *Slave Counterpoint*, 657–58). Pinn, *Varieties of African American Religious Experience*, 6; Orser, "The Archaeology of African-American Slave Religion in the Antebellum South," 35–36; Morgan, *Slave Counterpoint*, 420; Pinn, *Varieties of African American Religious Experience*, 7; Charles W. Joyner, *Down by the Riverside*, 143; Long, "Perspectives for a Study of African-American Religion in the United States," in Fulop and Raboteau, *African-American Re-*

ligion: Interpretive Essays in History and Culture, 26; Alho, *The Religion of the Slaves,* 157, 167, 216; Williams, *Sunshine and Shadow of Slave Life,* 70 (Isaac Williams).

5. Joyner, *Down by the Riverside,* 144; Washington, *Frustrated Fellowship,* 108; Montgomery, *Under Their Own Vine and Fig Tree,* 257–64; Walker, *A Rock in a Weary Land,* 91; Phillip Shaw Paludan, "Religion and the American Civil War," in Miller, Stout, and Wilson, *Religion and the American Civil War,* 34; Federal Writers' Project, *Born in Slavery: Slave Narratives from the Federal Writers' Project, 1936–38,* Texas Narratives, Vol. 16, pt. 2 (Federal Writers' Project, United States Work Progress Administration, Manuscript Division, Library of Congress), 83, http://memory.loc.gov/ammem/snhtml/snhome.html (Austin Grant); Epstein, "Slave Music in the United States before 1860," 207; Marsden, *Fundamentalism and American Culture,* 11; Charles Reagan Wilson, "Religion and the American Civil War in Comparative Perspective," in Miller, Stout, and Wilson, *Religion and the American Civil War,* 396–97.

6. Fountain, "Historians and Historical Archaeology," 66–77. Archaeologists drew a similar conclusion based on their findings on a Louisiana sugar plantation (Yakubik, "Archaeological Data Recovery at Ashland-Belle Helene Plantation," 12–8). Leone and Fry, "Conjuring in the Big House," 372–403; Creel, *A Peculiar People,* 260; Genovese, *Roll, Jordan, Roll,* 610; C. C. Jones, *The Religious Instruction of the Negroes,* 110.

7. Sernett, *Black Religion and American Evangelicalism,* 164; Ross, *Slavery Ordained of God;* Sawyer, *Southern Institutions;* Johnson, *Drums and Shadows,* vii.

8. Yakubik, "Archaeological Data Recovery at Ashland-Belle Helene Plantation," chap. 8, p. 71, chap. 12, p. 9; Patten, "Mankala and Minkisi," 5–7; Russell, "Material Culture and African-American Spirituality at the Hermitage," 65; Orser, "The Archaeology of African-American Slave Religion in the Antebellum South," 42.

9. Reis, *Slave Rebellion in Brazil,* 106.

10. Austin, *African Muslims in Antebellum America: Transatlantic Stories and Spiritual Struggles, and African Muslims in Antebellum America: A Sourcebook;* Gomez, *Exchanging Our Country Marks,* and "Muslims in Early America," 671–710; Diouf, *Servants of Allah.*

11. See Diouf, *Servants of Allah,* 52–59; Austin, *African Muslims in Antebellum America: A Sourcebook,* 121–264; Hefner, "World Building and the Rationality of Conversion," in *Conversion to Christianity,* 16.

12. Gomez, "Muslims in Early America," 671–710; Martin, "Sapelo Island's Arabic Document," 589–601; Austin, *African Muslims: A Sourcebook,* 309–408. Charles Joyner writes of rice planters who used beef instead of pork for rations for their Muslim slaves (Joyner, *Down by the Riverside,* 171). Gomez, "Muslims in Early America," 671–710. See also Rawick, *American Slave,* Series 1, South Carolina, pts. 1 & 2, 2:163 (Solbert Butler).

13. Diouf, *Servants of Allah,* 69; Ferris, "Voodoo," in Wilson and Ferris, *Encyclopedia of Southern Culture,* 492; McKee, "The Earth Is Their Witness," 40; Russell, "Material Culture and African-American Spirituality at the Hermitage," 63–80 (for a discussion of other links between slave jewelry and possible Islamic connections, see Stine, Cabak, and Groover, "Blue Beads as African-American Cultural Symbols," 49–75); Reis, *Slave Rebellion in Brazil,* 102. See also Gomez, *Exchanging Our Country Marks,* 67; Diouf, *Servants of Allah,* 129–34.

14. Davis, *American Voudou,* ix–xii; Mulira, "The Case of Voodoo in New Orleans," in Holloway, *Africanisms in American Culture,* 34; Ferris, "Voodoo," 492; Gomez, *Exchanging*

Our Country Marks, 57; Diouf, *Servants of Allah,* 180; Gomez, *Exchanging Our Country Marks,* 79.

15. Gomez, *Exchanging Our Country Marks,* 56; Pinn, *Varieties of African American Religious Experience,* 11–34; Barrett, "The African Heritage," 181; Hurston, *Mules and Men,* 207–27; Gomez, *Exchanging Our Country Marks,* 55–56.

16. Mulira, "The Case of Voodoo in New Orleans," in Holloway, *Africanisms in American Culture,* 34; Ferris, "Voodoo," 492; Gomez, *Exchanging Our Country Marks,* 56–57; Bodin, *Voodoo, Past and Present,* 9; Pinn, *Varieties of African American Religious Experience,* 12; Mulira, "The Case of Voodoo in New Orleans," in Holloway, *Africanisms in American Culture,* 37.

17. Deren, *Divine Horsemen,* 54–61; Metraux, *Voodoo in Haiti,* 28, 323–35; Pinn, *Varieties of African American Religious Experience,* 20–23.

18. Pinn, *Varieties of African American Religious Experience,* 34–35; Mulira, "The Case of Voodoo in New Orleans," in Holloway, *Africanisms in American Culture,* 35; Raboteau, *Slave Religion,* 80; Bruce, *The New Man,* 58.

19. Voeks, "African Medicine and Magic in the Americas," 71; Mulira, "The Case of Voodoo in New Orleans," in Holloway, *Africanisms in American Culture,* 49–56; Ferris, "Voodoo," 492; Raboteau, *Slave Religion,* 79; Ferris, "Voodoo," 492; Rod Davis, *American Voudou.*

20. See Mbiti, *African Religions and Philosophy* and *Introduction to African Religion;* Parrinder, *African Traditional Religion;* Raboteau, *Slave Religion,* 43–92; Sobel, *Trabelin' On,* 3–75, 122–25; Genovese, *Roll, Jordan, Roll,* 209–17; Young, "Archaeological Evidence of African-Style Ritual and Healing Practices in the Upland South," 145–47; Charles H. Long, "Perspectives for a Study of African-American Religion in the United States," in Fulop and Raboteau, *African-American Religion: Interpretive Essays in History and Culture,* 25; Parrinder, *African Traditional Religion,* 11; Sidney W. Mintz and Richard Price, "The Birth of African-American Culture," in Fulop and Raboteau, *African-American Religion: Interpretive Essays in History and Culture,* 41; Coleman, *Tribal Talk,* 31–34; Mbiti, *Introduction to African Religion,* 17 (see also Zahan, *The Religion, Spirituality and Thought of Traditional Africa;* Houk, "Anthropological Theory and the Breakdown of Eclectic Folk Religions," 442; Herskovits, *The Myth of the Negro Past,* 141–42, 296–98); Mbiti, *African Religions and Philosophy,* 5; Patten, "Mankala and Minkisi," 6.

21. Gomez, *Exchanging Our Country Marks,* 256; Emefie Ikenga-Metuh, "The Shattered Microcosm: A Critical Survey of Explanations of Conversion in Africa," in Petersen, *Religion, Development, and African Identity,* 26; Oates, *The Fires of Jubilee,* 49–50; Clendinnen, *Ambivalent Conquests,* 165.

22. Long, "Perspectives for a Study of African-American Religion in the United States," in Fulop and Raboteau, *African-American Religion: Interpretive Essays in History and Culture,* 26. See also Frey and Wood, *Come Shouting to Zion,* 35. Frey and Wood argue against Jon Butler's notion of an African spiritual holocaust. They argue that while some survivors of the middle passage may have lost faith in their traditional faiths, "the majority did not." Mintz and Price, "The Birth of African-American Culture," in Fulop and Raboteau, *African-American Religion: Interpretive Essays in History and Culture,* 43–44; Karen McCarthy Brown, "Systematic Remembering, Systematic Forgetting: Ogou in Haiti," in Fulop and Raboteau, *African-American Religion: Interpretive Essays in History and Culture,* 436; Coleman, *Tribal Talk,* 34. This proposed model for religious adaptation

relies heavily on the pattern of cultural development suggested by Mintz and Price in *The Birth of African-American Culture: An Anthropological Perspective.*

23. Alho, *The Religion of the Slaves,* 32; Du Bois, *The Souls of Black Folk,* 144–45; Russell, "Material Culture and African-American Spirituality at the Hermitage," 65; Gomez, *Exchanging Our Country Marks,* 272; Albert, *The House of Bondage,* 5, 23 (Charlotte Brooks); Bruce, *The New Man,* 58. Although Michael Gomez does not see conjure as evidence of a modified African religious belief system, he offers a similar interpretation of conjure as a spiritual worldview. See Gomez, *Exchanging Our Country Marks,* 284–89.

24. Ball, *Fifty Years in Chains,* 15, 198; Douglass, *Life and Times of Frederick Douglass,* 137; Harrison, *The Gospel among the Slaves,* 306; C. C. Jones, *The Religious Instruction of the Negroes,* 127–28; Wightman, *Life of William Capers,* 298–99.

25. Charles E. Orser, "The Archaeology of African American Slave Religion in the Antebellum South," in Conser and Payne, *Southern Crossroads,* 39–62; Ferguson, *Uncommon Ground,* 23; Hume, "An Indian Ware of the Colonial Period," 2–14. See also Fountain, "Historians and Historical Archaeology," 66–77.

26. Ferguson, *Uncommon Ground,* 117; Samford, "Searching for West African Cultural Meanings in the Archaeological Record," 3; Deetz, *Flowerdew Hundred,* 78–90; Pogue and White, "Summary Report on the 'House for Families' Slave Quarter Site," 203; Polehmus, "Archaeological Investigation of the Tellico Blockhouse Site," 314. See also Fountain, "Historians and Historical Archaeology," 66–77.

27. Ferguson, *Uncommon Ground,* 114. See also Fountain, "Historians and Historical Archaeology," 66–77.

28. Ferguson, *Uncommon Ground,* 114–16. See also Fountain, "Historians and Historical Archaeology," 66–77.

29. Ascher and Fairbanks, "Excavation of a Slave Cabin: Georgia, USA," 8–9; Brown and Cooper, "Structural Continuity in an African-American Slave and Tenant Community," 7–19; Handler, Lange, and Orser, "Carnelian Beads in Necklaces from a Slave Cemetery in Barbados, West Indies," 15–18; Pogue and White, "Summary Report on the 'House for Families' Slave Quarter Site," 200; Stine, Cabak, and Groover, "Blue Beads as African-American Cultural Symbols," 49–75; Chireau, "Conjure and Christianity in the Nineteenth Century," 228; Singleton, "The Archaeology of Slavery in North America," 130–31; Young, "Archaeological Evidence of African-Style Ritual and Healing Practices in the Upland South," 149; Orser, "The Archaeology of African American Slave Religion in the Antebellum South," in Conser and Payne, *Southern Crossroads,* 39–62. John Mbiti shows that such personal decorations are still used in Africa for controlling evil spirits (Mbiti, *Introduction to African Religion,* 80).

30. Ferguson, *Uncommon Ground,* 114–16; Patten, "Mankala and Minkisi," 5–7; Wilkie, "Magic and Empowerment on the Plantation," 136–48; Young, "Archaeological Evidence of African-Style Ritual and Healing Practices in the Upland South," 131, 145–46; Yakubik, "Archaeological Data Recovery at Ashland-Belle Helene Plantation," chap. 10, 71–75; Brown and Cooper, "Structural Continuity in an African-American Slave and Tenant Community," 7–19; Singleton, "The Archaeology of Slavery in North America," 131; Adams, "Religion and Freedom," 8.

31. Sobel, *Trabelin' On,* 41 (see also Joyner, *Down by the Riverside,* 141–71; Raboteau, *Slave Religion,* 275–88; Lawrence Levine, *Black Culture and Black Consciousness,* 55–80;

Du Bois, *The Souls of Black Folk,* 146; Zipf, "'Among These American Heathens,'" 123); Chireau, *Black Magic,* 4. Numerous other scholars join Lawrence Levine in describing the belief in the power of magic, divination, and ritual dance in terms of religion (see also Camara, "Afro-American Religious Syncretism," 299–318; Thomas Leonard Williams, "The Methodist Mission to the Slaves" (PhD diss., Yale University, 1976), 74–80; Hefner, "World Building and the Rationality of Conversion," 3–46; Mbiti, *African Religions and Philosophy,* 233; Wilkie, "Magic and Empowerment on the Plantation," 136–48); Genovese, *Roll, Jordan, Roll,* 217. Donald G. Mathews agrees with this assessment (Mathews, *Religion in the Old South,* 209–10; see also Anderson, *Conjure in African American Society,* 3). Orser, "The Archaeology of African American Slave Religion in the Antebellum South," in Conser and Payne, *Southern Crossroads,* 44.

32. Morgan, *Slave Counterpoint,* 611; Coleman, *Tribal Talk,* 34; Horton, *Patterns of Thought,* 373; Mbiti, *Introduction to African Religion,* 41–42; Herskovits, *The Myth of the Negro Past,* 237; Hyatt, *Hoodoo-Conjuration-Witchcraft-Rootwork,* 76, 78–82; Johnson, *Drums and Shadows,* 29; Waters, *Strange Ways and Sweet Dreams,* 136, 227, 280; Brown, "Conjure/Doctors," 10–11; Robinson, "Black Healers," 77; Chireau, *Black Magic,* 4–7.

33. Gaustad, *A Documentary History of Religion in America,* 2–3. See also Byrne, "Folklore and the Study of American Religion," in Lippy and Williams, *Encyclopedia of the American Religious Experience,* 85–100. Byrne defines folk religion as "traditional, informal religious culture, sometimes involving survivals or syncretism, endlessly adopted to new situations." Catherine Albanese also offers a definition of religion that would embrace the slaves' spiritual activities as religious (Albanese, *America: Religions and Religion,* 8–10).

34. Levine, *Black Culture and Black Consciousness,* 58.

35. Johnson, *Twenty-Eight Years a Slave in Virginia,* 10 (Thomas Johnson); Ball, *Fifty Years in Chains,* 193 (Charles Ball); Grimes, *The Life of William Grimes,* 15, 23–25 (William Grimes); Rawick, *American Slave,* Series 1, Alabama and Indiana, 6:70 (Henry Cheatam), Series 2, North Carolina, 15:121 (Patsy Mitchner), Series 2, North Carolina, 15:361 (Ellen Trell), Series 1, South Carolina, pts. 3 & 4, 3:6 (Sam Rawls), Series 1, South Carolina, pts. 1 & 2, 2:2 (M. E. Abrams).

36. Mbiti, *African Religions and Philosophy,* 203–12; Rawick, *American Slave,* Series 1, South Carolina, pts. 1 & 2, 2:130 (John C. Brown); C. C. Jones, *The Religious Instruction of the Negroes in the United States,* 125; Morgan, *Slave Counterpoint,* 635.

37. Genovese, *Roll, Jordan, Roll,* 215; Levine, *Black Culture and Black Consciousness,* 55–80; Zipf, "'Among These American Heathens,'" 123; Brown, *My Southern Home,* 59–70 (William Wells Brown); Hughes, *Thirty Years a Slave,* 108 (Louis Hughes); Bibb, *Narrative of the Life and Adventures of Henry Bibb,* 25 (Henry Bibb); Douglass, *Narrative of the Life of Frederick Douglass,* 80 (Frederick Douglass); Bruce, *The New Man,* 52 (Henry Bruce).

38. Du Bois, *The Souls of Black Folk,* 144. For studies addressing conjure ritual, see Puckett, *Folk Beliefs of the Southern Negro;* Hyatt, *Hoodoo-Conjuration-Witchcraft-Rootwork;* Johnson, *Drums and Shadows,* vii; Waters, *Strange Ways and Sweet Dreams;* Rawick, *American Slave,* Series 1, Texas, pts. 3 & 4, 4:216 (Jenny Proctor); Douglass, *Narrative of the Life of Frederick Douglass,* 70; Hughes, *Thirty Years a Slave,* 108 (Louis Hughes); Federal Writers' Project, *Born in Slavery: Slave Narratives from the Federal Writers' Project, 1936–38,* Alabama Narratives, vol. 1 (Federal Writers Project, United States Work Prog-

ress Administration, Manuscript Division, Library of Congress), 430, http://memory
.loc.gov/ammem/snhtml/snhome.html (Silvia Witherspoon), Oklahoma Narratives, vol.
13, 245 (Henry Pyles), and Georgia Narratives, vol. 4, pt. 4, 261 (George Leonard).

39. Wilkie, "Magic and Empowerment on the Plantation," 137; Gorn, "Black Spirits:
the Ghostlore of African American Slaves," 4; Morgan, *Slave Counterpoint,* 631; Du Bois,
The Souls of Black Folk, 146; Sernett, *Black Religion and American Evangelicalism,* 61; C. C.
Jones, *The Religious Instruction of the Negroes,* 128; Wightman, *Life of William Capers,* 116.

40. Robert L. Hall, "African Religious Retentions in Florida," in Holloway, *Africanisms
in American Culture,* 112–13; Frey and Wood, *Come Shouting to Zion,* 51–53; Alho, *The Religion of the Slaves,* 161–63; George Brandon, "Sacrificial Practices in Santeria, an African-
Cuban Religion in the United States," in Holloway, *Africanisms in American Culture,* 141
(see also Mbiti, *Introduction to African Religion,* 18); Vlach, *The Afro-American Tradition in Decorative Arts,* 139–47; Thompson, *Flash of the Spirit,* 135–45 (see also Margaret
Washington Creel, "Gullah Attitudes toward Life and Death," in Holloway, *Africanisms
in American Culture,* 69–97; Gomez, *Exchanging Our Country Marks,* 275; Gorn, "Black
Spirits: The Ghostlore of Afro-American Slaves," 549–65; Joyner, "History as Ritual," 3;
Johnson, *Drums and Shadows,* 62).

41. Ephesians 2:8–9.

42. Raboteau, *Slave Religion,* 288. See also Chireau, "Conjure and Christianity in the
Nineteenth Century," 226–46; Genovese, *Roll, Jordan, Roll,* 217.

43. Chireau, *Black Magic,* 11–34.

44. Heyrman, *Southern Cross,* 49–52; Johnson and Jersild, *"Ain't Gonna Lay My 'Ligion Down"*; Earl, *Dark Symbols, Obscure Signs: God, Self, and Community in the Slave Mind.*

45. C. C. Jones, *The Religious Instruction of the Negroes,* 125.

46. Travis, *Rev. Joseph Travis, A.M., a Member of the Memphis Annual Conference,* 71–72.

47. Du Bois, *The Souls of Black Folk,* 146. See also Albanese, *A Republic of Mind and
Spirit,* 93–95.

48. Rawick, *American Slave,* Series 1, Alabama and Indiana, 6:36 (Ank Bishop); Saxon,
Dreyer, and Tallant, *Gumbo Ya-Ya,* 243 (Elizabeth Hite); Rawick, *American Slave,* Series 1,
South Carolina, pts. 1 & 2, 2:139 (Sara Brown), Supp. Series 2, Texas, pt. 1, 2:369 (James
Boyd), Series 2, Georgia, pt. 1 & 2, 12:245 (Martha Colquitt).

4. CHRIST UNCHAINED

1. C. C. Jones, *Religious Instruction of the Negroes: An Address,* 12; Montgomery, *Under Their Own Vine and Fig Tree,* 40.

2. Sernett, *Black Religion and American Evangelicalism,* 85; Rawick, *American Slave,*
Series 2, Kansas et al., 16:116 (William Williams; see also Rawick, *American Slave,* Series
2, Arkansas, pts. 1 & 2, 8:282 [George Brown]; Clayton, *Mother Wit,* 44, 84 [Manda Coo-
per, Ceceil George]; Rawick, *American Slave,* Series 2, Kansas et al., 16:38 [Mary James]);
Thomas Jones, *The Experience of Thomas H. Jones,* 25 (see also Rawick, *American Slave,*
Supp. Series 1, Mississippi, pt. 1, 6:202 [Aunt Dora]); Jackson, *The Experience of a Slave
in South Carolina,* 8 (John Andrew Jackson; see also Rawick, *American Slave,* Series 2,
Florida, 17:166 [Charlotte Martin]; Grandy, *Narrative of the Life of Moses Grandy,* 35;

Rawick, *American Slave*, Series 2, Kansas et al., 16:31 [Rev. Silas Jackson]; "Report of Mr. S. G. Wright, Van Buren Camp, Louisiana, January 1864," *Eighteenth Annual Report of the American Missionary Association* [New York: American Missionary Association, 1864], 20; Raboteau, *Slave Religion*, 307–8); "Report of Mr. S. G. Wright, Van Buren Camp, Louisiana, January 1864," *Eighteenth Annual Report of the American Missionary Association* (New York: American Missionary Association, 1864), 20.

3. For scripture on the value of human life, see 1 Corinthians 12:12–13; 1 Timothy 4:4; Luke 12:24; Matthew 10:29–30. For scripture on the spiritual equality of humanity, see 2 Corinthians 5:10; Hebrews 9:27–28; Romans 13:10–12. For scripture on the reasons for Jesus's death, see Romans 3:23–26; John 3:16, 5:24. For scripture on the promise of eternal life, see Romans 5:1–3; Acts 17:31; 2 Timothy 4:1; John 16:20; Isaiah 42:1; Romans 13:17; Matthew 11:28–30.

4. Raboteau, "African-Americans, Exodus, and the American Israel," in Paul Johnson, *African-American Christianity*, 13 (see also Katharine L. Dvorak, "After Apocalypse, Moses," in Boles, *Masters & Slaves in the House of the Lord*, 175; Sobel *Trabelin' On*, 125; Smith, "Religion and Ethnicity in America," *American Historical Review* 83 [December 1978]: 1182; Genovese, *Roll, Jordan, Roll*, 253–54); Williams, *Narrative of James Williams*, 73–74; Rawick, *American Slave*, Series 1, Alabama and Indiana, 6:416 (Mingo White), and Supp. Series 1, Indiana and Ohio, 5:48 (Robert J. Cheatham; see also Rawick, *American Slave*, Series 1, Alabama and Indiana, 56 [James Childress]; Furman, *Slavery in the Clover Bottoms*, 48; New England Educational Commission, *Extracts from Letters of Teachers and Superintendents of the New England Educational Commission for Freedmen*, Fourth Series [Boston: David Clapp, 1864], 8; Cimprich, "Slave Behavior during the Federal Occupation of Tennessee," 338); Rawick, *American Slave*, Series 1, South Carolina, pts. 3 & 4, 3:260 (Victoria Perry). And see also Rawick, *American Slave*, Supp. Series 1, Indiana and Ohio, 142–43 (John Moore); Rawick, *American Slave*, Series 2, North Carolina, pt. 2, 15:130 (Fannie Moore).

5. Rawick, *American Slave*, Series 2, Georgia, pts. 1 & 2, 12:26 (Mary Gladdy; see also Rawick, *American Slave*, Series 2, Florida, 17:291 [William Sherman], Supp. Series 1, Mississippi, pt. 2, 7:785 [Dora Franks]), Series 1, South Carolina, pts.. 1 & 2, 2:285 (Maria Heywood), Supp. Series 1, Mississippi, pt. 1, 6:249 (Ebenezer Brown), Series 2, North Carolina, pt. 2, 15:56 (Channa Littlejohn), and Series 1, Alabama and Indiana, 6:427 (Callie Williams; and see also Rawick, *American Slave*, Series 2, Kansas et al., 16:49 [Andrew Moss]; Raboteau, *Slave Religion*, 308–9), Series 2, Arkansas, pts. 5 & 6, 10:64 (Tom Robinson).

6. Rawick, *American Slave*, Series 1, Alabama and Indiana, 6:422 (Mingo White), and Supp. Series 1, Indiana and Ohio, 5:49 (Robert J. Cheatham); Robinson, *From Log Cabin to the Pulpit*, 36; Rawick, *American Slave*, Series 1, South Carolina, pts. 3 & 4, 3:45–47 (Reuben Rosborough); Edward L. Pierce, "The Contrabands at Fortress Monroe," *Atlantic Monthly* 8 (November 1861): 638; Cimprich, "Slave Behavior during the Federal Occupation of Tennessee," 338; Rawick, *American Slave*, Series 1, Texas, pts. 1 & 2, 4:92 (O. W. Green), and Series 2, Florida, 142 (Clayborn Gantling; see also Rawick, *American Slave*, Series 1, South Carolina, pts. 3 & 4, 3:260–61 [Victoria Perry], Series 2, North Carolina, pts. 2, 428 [Dilly Yellasy], Series 2, Arkansas, pts. 5 & 6, 10:64 [Tom Robinson], and Series 2, Fisk Narratives, 18:17 [White Folks Pet]; "Anecdote and Incidents of a Visit

to Freedmen," *Freedmen's Record* [October 1865]): 158; Albert, *The House of Bondage*, 55 (Charlotte Brooks); Blassingame, *Slave Testimony*, 504 (L. M. Mills); Rawick, *American Slave*, Series 2, Fisk Narratives, 18:259 (All My Bosses Were Nigger Traders).

7. Rawick, *American Slave*, Supp. Series 1, Mississippi, pts. 2, 7:671 (Mollie Edmonds), Series 2, Kansas et al., 109 (Julia Williams); Blassingame, *Slave Testimony*, 660–61 (Henry Baker); Rawick, *American Slave*, Series 2, Florida, 17:160 (Harriett Gresham), and Series 1, South Carolina, pts. 3 & 4, 3:37 (Charlie Robinson; see also Rawick, *American Slave*, Supp. Series 2, Texas, pt. 7, 8:3398 [Peter Ryas]; Drago, "How Sherman's March through Georgia Affected the Slaves," 364).

8. Rawick, *American Slave*, Series 1, Alabama and Indiana, 6:188 (Barney Stone), Series 2, Fisk Narratives, 19:120 (Slave Who Joined the Yanks), Supp. Series 1, Mississippi, pt. 3, 8:1221–23 (Julius Jones); Harris, *"In the Country of the Enemy,"* 171 (entry for May 12, 1863).

9. McWhiney, Moore, and Pace, *"Fear God and Walk Humbly,"* 310, 313, 391 (entries for August 17, 1862; October 19, 1862; August 9, 1868; August 26–27, 1868).

10. Given the deep religious nature of the missionaries to the freedmen, the author tends to trust that their reports of conversions are accurate. However, it is important to note that a missionary's job and reputation hinged on his success in converting the targeted population.

11. American Missionary Association, *Sixteenth Annual Report of the American Missionary Association* (New York: American Missionary Association, 1862), 41, 43, 53–54. See also "Anecdote and Incidents of a Visit to Freedmen," *Freedmen's Record* (October 1865): 158.

12. At least two former slaves who left narratives attributed their conversion to the efforts of missionaries sent to the South during or after the Civil War (Ferebee, *A Brief History of the Slave Life of Rev. L. R. Ferebee*, 10; Blassingame, *Slave Testimony*, 610 [Harry Jarvis]).

13. Forten, "Life on the Sea Islands," in *Two Black Teachers during the Civil War*, 80. See also Pearson, *Letters from Port Royal, 1862–1868*, 145.

14. American Missionary Association, *Seventeenth Annual Report of the American Missionary Association* (New York: American Missionary Association, 1863), 40–41.

15. Ibid., 47. See also ibid., 37–39 (entries for Fortress Monroe, Newport News, Portsmouth).

16. American Missionary Association, *Eighteenth Annual Report of the American Missionary Association* (New York: American Missionary Association, 1864), 14.

17. Ibid., 12, 21, 22. For evidence of frequent conversions and revivals among African Americans, see also ibid., 42–43 (entries for South Carolina, Missouri); American Missionary Association, *Nineteenth Annual Report of the American Missionary Association* (New York: American Missionary Association, 1865): 17, 26, 27–28, 33 (entries for Washington, DC, Florida, Kansas, and Missouri, Port Hudson, Mississippi); American Missionary Association, *Twentieth Annual Report of the American Missionary Association* (New York: American Missionary Association, 1866), 22, 26, 39 (entries for Fortress Monroe, Roanoke Island, Kentucky); "Work of a Colored Chaplain in North Carolina," *The Independent*, June 1, 1865, 4 (Goldsboro, NC); "Letter from Charleston," *Christian Advocate*, January 11, 1866, 1.

18. "Letter to George Whipple from Rev. A. D. Olds, June 7th? 1863," *American Missionary Association Manuscripts from the Amistad Collection* (microfilm), Mississippi Roll No. 1, Manuscript No. 1551. See also Walker, "Corinth: The Story of a Contraband Camp," 13.

19. American Missionary Association, *Nineteenth Annual Report of the American Missionary Association*, 33.

20. Reilly, *Sarah Jane Foster*, 46, 54–55, 70, 129.

21. "M. E. Church South," *Christian Advocate*, January 11, 1866, 1; American Missionary Association, *Twentieth Annual Report of the American Missionary Association*, 22; Jamison, *Autobiography and Work of Bishop M. F. Jamison*, 47; McCray, *Life of Mary F. McCray*, 39–40; Smith, *A History of the African Methodist Episcopal Church*, 504.

22. Shattuck, *A Shield and Hiding Place*, 73–110; Ahlstrom, *A Religious History of the American People*, 674–78. See also Miller, Stout, and Wilson, *Religion and the American Civil War*; Armstrong, *For Courageous Fighting and Confident Dying*; William Jones, *Christ in the Camp*.

23. Shattuck, *A Shield and Hiding Place*, 81, 89, 92; Ahlstrom, *A Religious History of the American People*, 677; Harris, *"In the Country of the Enemy,"* 171 (entry for May 12, 1863); Johnson, *Twenty-Eight Years a Slave in Virginia*, 47; Marrs, *The Life of John Thompson*, 24.

24. Redkey, "Black Chaplains in the Union Army," 339–40; Higginson, *Army Life in a Black Regiment*, 255–56.

25. American Missionary Association, *Nineteenth Annual Report of the American Missionary Association*, 33.

26. American Missionary Association, *Twenty-First Annual Report of the American Missionary Association*, 27.

27. American Missionary Association, *Twenty-Fourth Annual Report of the American Missionary Association*, 32.

28. Katharine L. Dvorak, "After Apocalypse, Moses," in Boles, *Masters & Slaves in the House of the Lord*, 173–91; Stowell, *Rebuilding Zion*, 70–71, 90; Montgomery, *Under Their Own Vine and Fig Tree*, 59–71. See also Walker, *A Rock in a Weary Land*, 80; Taylor, *Louisiana Reconstructed, 1863–1877*, 129, 453; Owen, *The Sacred Flame of Love*, 129; Du Bois, *The Souls of Black Folk*, 142–44; Ahlstrom, *A Religious History of the American People*, 709.

29. American Missionary Association, *Nineteenth Annual Report of the American Missionary Association*, 13.

30. "Letter from Rev. G. W. Carruthers to Rev. S. S. Jocelyn, June 13, 1863," *American Missionary Association Manuscripts from the Amistad Collection* (microfilm), Mississippi, Roll No. 1, Manuscript No. 71552. See also "Letter from Rev. Ed. R. Pierce to Rev. S. S. Jocelyn, April 24, 1863," *American Missionary Association Manuscripts from the Amistad Collection* (microfilm), Mississippi, Roll No. 1, Manuscript No. 71545.

31. Christian aid societies like the AMA attempted to provide all families with copies of the Bible. For example, in 1863 the AMA mission at Fortress Monroe reported that "[t]he children have all been supplied with Testaments, and all the families have nearly all been visited and presented with Bibles" (American Missionary Association, *Seventeenth Annual Report of the American Missionary Association*, 37).

32. Sobel, *Trabelin' On*, 182; Raboteau, *Slave Religion*, 209; Owen, *The Sacred Flame of Love*, 129. Gunnar Myrdal draws the same conclusion about a wave of African Ameri-

can conversions following the Civil War (Myrdal, *An American Dilemma*, 860); Southern Baptist Convention, *Proceedings of the Southern Baptist Convention Eighth Biennial Session* (Richmond: 1861), 57, in Southern Baptist Historical Library and Archives, Nashville, Tennessee; General Missionary Baptist Association of Tennessee, *Minutes of the Second Annual Session of the General Missionary Baptist Association of Tennessee* (Memphis: Post Book and Print Office, 1869), unnumbered statistical appendix, in Southern Baptist Historical Library and Archives, Nashville, Tennessee.

33. For statistics on Georgia congregants, see Owen, *The Sacred Flame of Love*, 190 (app. 2), and Stowell, *Rebuilding Zion*, 80–83, 90. Walker, *A Rock in a Weary Land*, 71–72; Bouriaque, "A History of the Ouachita Baptist Association," 64; Greene, *House upon a Rock*, 176 (see also Hicks, *History of Louisiana Negro Baptists*, 53–55 [Hicks's research found that Louisiana's African American Baptists grew from 5,000 in 1867 to 125,000 by 1902]); Paxton, *A History of the Baptists of Louisiana*, 137; Bethel Baptist Institutional Church, *Souvenir Centennial Celebration Bethel Baptist Institutional Church, Golden Jubilee* (Jacksonville, FL, 1938), 5.

34. Middleton, *Directory and Pre-1900 Historical Survey of South Carolina's Black Baptists*, 2, 11, 12, 14, 32, 34, 53, 63, 72, 73, 78, 80, 136.

35. Wheeler, "Beyond One Man," 309–19; Washington, *Frustrated Fellowship*, xi (W. E. B. Du Bois also emphasizes the importance of freedom for faith [Du Bois, *The Souls of Black Folk*, 18]); Hicks, *History of Louisiana Negro Baptists*, 53–54; Rawick, *American Slave*, Series 1, Alabama and Indiana, 6:188 (Barney Stone; in listing his reasons for becoming a preacher, Stone acknowledged his "gratefulness to God for my deliverance and my salvation"); Perdue, *Weevils in the Wheat*, 184–85 (Beverly Jones).

36. Raboteau, *Slave Religion*, 313; Ball, *Fifty Years in Chains*, 32.

37. The quantitative data from chap. 1 demonstrated that 56.8 percent of urban slaves converted to Christianity while only 38 percent of rural slaves did so. See chap. 1 for further details.

38. Douglass, *Narrative of the Life of Frederick Douglass*, 79, 82–83, 142–43.

39. Kolchin, *American Slavery*, 178.

40. Philip D. Morgan also found this to be true of eighteenth-century slaves. Morgan notes, "Urban slaves were certainly more assimilated than their rural counterpoints and were thereby responsive to evangelicals; but, even more to the point, they were much less easily controlled by their masters" (Morgan, *Slave Counterpoint*, 435).

41. Scott quoted in DeBoer, *His Truth Is Marching On*, 269–71.

42. Charles Smith, *A History of the African Methodist Episcopal Church*, 126.

43. Cornelius, *Slave Missions and the Black Church in the Antebellum South*, 203; Higginbotham, *Righteous Discontent*, 19.

44. Smith, *A History of the African Methodist Episcopal Church*, 127.

45. Strieby quoted in DeBoer, *His Truth is Marching On*, 269–71. See also Higginbotham, *Righteous Discontent*, 43.

46. A Teacher in the South, "What Shall We Believe about the Negro?" *American Missionary* 45, no. 9 (September 1891), 316–18.

47. Smith, *A History of the African Methodist Episcopal Church*, 126; "Studies in the South" (author unknown), 479.

48. William Thomas, *The American Negro*, 156–57. For more on Thomas and his con-

troversial views on the freedmen, see John David Smith, *Black Judas: William Hannibal Thomas and "The American Negro."*

49. Harvey. "These Untutored Masses," in *Southern Crossroads,* 250; Washington, "The Awakening of the Negro," *Atlantic Monthly* 78, no. 467 (September 1896): 324; Washington, "The Colored Ministry: Its Defects and Needs," *Christian Union* 42 (August 14, 1890): 199–200 (see also Sehat, "The Civilizing Mission of Booker T. Washington," *Journal of Southern History* 73, no. 2 [May 2007]: 323–62); Du Bois, "Religion in the South," in Washington and Du Bois, *The Negro in the South,* 175, and *The Souls of Black Folk,* 17, 21–22; see also an article by the president of Fisk University: Cravath, "The Necessity of Endowing Our Larger Institutions," *American Missionary* 40, no. 11 [November 1886]: 316–19; Hildebrand, *The Times Were Strange and Stirring,* 33). Not all African American leaders shared Du Bois and Washington's criticism of black clergy. See Martin, *For God and Race,* 151–56; Angell, *Bishop Henry McNeal Turner and African-American Religion in the South.*

50. Higginbotham, *Righteous Discontent,* 44; Harvey, *Freedom's Coming,* 120; Anderson, *Conjure in African American Society,* 2; Chireau, *Black Magic,* 129; Cable, "Creole Slave Songs," *Century Magazine* 31, no. 6 (April 1886): 825; see also Cable, "Creole Slave Dances: The Dance in Place Congo," *Century Magazine* 31, no. 4 [February 1886]: 517–32; Tylor, "On the Survival of Savage Thought in Modern Civilization, Part I," *Appleton's Journal* 1, no. 18 [July 1869]: 566–68; Handy, "Witchcraft among the Negroes," *Appleton's Journal* 8, no. 194 [December 1872], 666–67; S. M. P., "Voodooism in Tennessee," *Atlantic Monthly* 64, no. 383 [September 1889], 376–80; Thanet, "Plantation Life in Arkansas," *Atlantic Monthly* 68, no. 405 [July 1891]: 32–49; *New York Times* articles: "Superstitious Negroes," October 1, 1891, 10, and "Old South Voodoism," November 18, 1894, 20); Anderson, *Conjure in African American Society,* 5; *North American Review* 128, no. 268 (March 1879): 225–84. See Chireau, *Black Magic;* Anderson, *Conjure in African American Society.*

51. Horton, *Patterns of Thought,* 45; Hampton students cited in Anderson, *Conjure in African American Society,* 3, and Chireau, *Black Magic,* 131–32; Warner, *Studies in the South and West and Comments on Canada,* 65 (see also Bodin, *Voodoo, Past and Present,* 25-27; *New York Times* articles: "The Voodoo Doctor Failed," July 1, 1886, 3, "A Voodoo Doctor in Trouble," August 15, 1887, 2, "He Obeyed the Voodoo," July 24, 1887, 3, "Dead in a Hoodoo Doctor's Office," August 12, 1899, 3, "Magic Was His Medicine," July 6, 1896, 9, "Killed by a Voodoo Doctor," November 26, 1892, 6, and "Hanged as a Voodoo," December 11, 1887, 2). For the decline of non-Christian traditions among the freedmen, see Levine, *Black Culture and Black Consciousness,* 162; Montgomery, *Under Their Own Vine and Fig Tree,* 261–64; Du Bois, *The Souls of Black Folk,* 142–48; Boothe, *The Cyclopedia of the Colored Baptists of Alabama* (Boothe specifically wrote this book to outline the great religious changes that occurred within the African American community during the three decades after emancipation); Bruce, *The New Man,* 52; Du Bois, *The Souls of Black Folk,* 142.

CONCLUSION

1. Gomez, *Exchanging Our Country Marks,* 82; Diouf, *Servants of Allah,* 91.

2. Perdue,*Weevils in the Wheat,* 100–103 (Cornelius Gardner); Alho, *The Religion of the Slaves,* 191.

SELECTED BIBLIOGRAPHY

Abrahams, Roger D. *Singing the Master: The Emergence of African-American Culture in the Plantation South*. New York: Penguin, 1992.

Adams, Eric. "Religion and Freedom: Artifacts Indicate That African Culture Persisted Even in Slavery." *Omni Magazine* 16 (November 1993): 8.

Ahlstrom, Sydney E. *A Religious History of the American People*. New Haven, CT: Yale University Press, 1972.

Albanese, Catherine. *America: Religions and Religion*. 3rd ed. Belmont, CA: Wadsworth, 1999.

———. *A Republic of Mind and Spirit: A Cultural History of American Metaphysical Religion*. New Haven, CT: Yale University Press, 2007.

Albert, Octavia V. Rogers. *The House of Bondage; or, Charlotte Brooks and Other Slaves*. New York: Oxford University Press, 1988.

Alho, Olli. *The Religion of the Slaves: A Study of the Religious Tradition and Behavior of Plantation Slaves in the United States, 1830–1865*. FF Communications No. 217. Helsinki: Academia Scientarium Fennica, 1980.

Ammerman, Nancy T. *Baptist Battles: Social Change and Religious Conflict in the South Baptist Convention*. New Brunswick, NJ: Rutgers University Press, 1990.

Anderson, Jeffrey E. *Conjure in African American Society*. Baton Rouge: Louisiana State University Press, 2005.

Angell, Stephen W. *Bishop Henry McNeal Turner and African-American Religion in the South*. Knoxville: University of Tennessee Press, 1992.

Armstrong, Warren B. *For Courageous Fighting and Confident Dying: Union Chaplains in the Civil War*. Lawrence: University Press of Kansas, 1998.

Ascher, Robert, and Charles Fairbanks. "Excavation of a Slave Cabin: Georgia, USA." *Historical Archaeology* 5 (1971): 3–17.

Austin, Allan D. *African Muslims in Antebellum America: A Sourcebook*. New York: Garland, 1984.

———. *African Muslims in Antebellum America: Transatlantic Stories and Spiritual Struggles*. New York: Routledge, 1997.

Bailey, David T. "A Divided Prism: Two Sources of Black Testimony on Slavery." *Journal of Southern History* 46 (August 1980): 381–404.

———. "Frontier Religion." In *Encyclopedia of Southern Culture,* ed. Charles Wilson and William Ferris, 1286–88. Chapel Hill: University of North Carolina Press, 1989.

Baker, Lindsay T., and Julie P. Baker, eds. *The WPA Oklahoma Slave Narratives.* Norman: University of Oklahoma Press, 1996.

Ball, Charles. *Fifty Years in Chains; or, The Life of an American Slave.* New York: H. Dayton, 1859.

Barrett, Leonard E. "The African Heritage in Caribbean and North American Religions." In *Encyclopedia of the American Religious Experience,* ed. Charles H. Lippy and Peters W. Williams, 171–86. New York: Scribner's, 1988.

Baudier, Rodger. *The Catholic Church in Louisiana.* 1939. Reprint. New Orleans: Louisiana Library Association, 1972.

Berndt, Thomas J. *Child Development.* Fort Worth, TX: Harcourt Brace Jovanovich, 1992.

Bibb, Henry. *Narrative of the Life and Adventures of Henry Bibb, an American Slave.* New York: Published by the Author, 1850.

Black, James Daryl. "Contours of Faith: An Intellectual and Social Profile of the Georgia Baptist Association, 1820–1860." Master's thesis, California State University, Long Beach, 1996.

Blassingame, John W. *Slave Testimony: Two Centuries of Letters, Speeches, Interviews, and Autobiographies.* Baton Rouge: Louisiana State University Press, 1977.

———. *The Slave Community: Plantation Life in the Antebellum South.* New York: Oxford University Press, 1979.

Bode, Fred. "The Formation of Evangelical Communities in Middle Georgia: Twiggs County, 1820–1861." *Journal of Southern History* 60 (1994): 711–48.

Bodin, Ron. *Voodoo: Past and Present.* Louisiana Life Series, No. 5. Lafayette: University of Southwestern Louisiana, 1990.

Boles, John. *Black Southerners, 1619–1869.* Lexington: University Press of Kentucky, 1983.

———, ed. *Masters & Slaves in the House of the Lord: Race and Religion in the American South, 1740–1870.* Lexington: University Press of Kentucky, 1988.

Boothe, Charles Octavius. *The Cyclopedia of the Colored Baptists of Alabama.* Birmingham: Alabama Publishing, 1895.

Bouriaque, Edward Lynn. "A History of the Ouachita Baptist Association during the Nineteenth Century." Master's thesis, Northwestern State University, Louisiana, 1971.

Breeden, James O. ed. *Advice among Masters: The Ideal in Slave Management in the Old South.* Westport, CT: Greenwood, 1980.

Brown, David H. "Conjure/Doctors: An Exploration of a Black Discourse in America, Antebellum to 1940." *Folklore Forum* 23 (1990): 3–46.

Brown, Kenneth, and Doreen Cooper. "Structural Continuity in an African-American Slave and Tenant Community." *Historical Archaeology* 24 (1990): 7–19.

Brown, William Wells. *Narrative of William Wells Brown: A Fugitive Slave*. Boston: Anti-Slavery Office, 1847.

———. *My Southern Home; or, The South and Its People*. Boston: A.G. Brown & Co., 1880.

Bruce, H. C. *The New Man: Twenty-Nine Years a Slave. Twenty-Nine Years a Free Man: Recollections of H. C. Bruce*. York, PA: P. Anstadt & Sons, 1895.

Butler, Jon. *Awash in a Sea of Faith: Christianizing the American People*. Cambridge, MA: Harvard University Press, 1990.

Butler, Kevin D. "The Creation of African American Christianity: Slavery and Religion in Antebellum Missouri." Dissertation, University of Missouri–Columbia, 2005.

Butt, Audrey J. "The Birth of a Religion." In *Gods and Rituals: Readings in Religious Beliefs and Practices,* ed. John Middleton, 377–435. Garden City, NY: Natural History Press, 1967.

Byrne, Donald E., Jr. "Folklore and the Study of American Religion." In *Encyclopedia of the American Religious Experience: Studies of Traditions and Movements,* vol. 1, ed. Charles H. Lippy and Peter W. Williams, 85–100. New York: Scribner's, 1988.

Cable, George Washington. "Creole Slave Dances: The Dance in Place Congo." *Century Magazine* 31, no. 4 (February 1886): 517–32.

———. "Creole Slave Songs." *Century Magazine* 31, no. 6 (April 1886): 807–28.

Cain, J. B. *Methodism in the Mississippi Conference, 1846–1870*. Jackson: Mississippi Conference Historical Society, 1939.

Camara, Evandro M. "Afro-American Religious Syncretism." *Sociological Analysis* 48 (1988): 299–318.

Capers, William. *A Catechism for Little Children, the Missions of the Methodist Episcopal Church in South Carolina*. Charleston, SC: J. S. Burges, 1833.

Carson, Clayborne, ed. *The Papers of Martin Luther King, Jr.,* vol. 1. Berkeley: University of California Press, 1992.

Chambliss, Alexander W. *The Catechetical Instructor*. Montgomery, AL: Bates, Hooper, & Company, 1847.

Cheesebrough, David B. *"God Ordained This War": Sermons on the Sectional Crisis, 1830–1865*. Columbia: University of South Carolina Press, 1991.

Chesnut, Mary Boykin. *A Diary from Dixie*. Ed. Ben Ames Williams. Boston: Houghton Mifflin, 1949.

Chireau, Yvonne. "Conjure and Christianity in the Nineteenth Century: Religious Elements in African American Magic." *Religion and American Culture* 7 (Summer 1997): 225–46.

————. *Black Magic: Religion and the African American Conjuring Tradition.* Berkeley: University of California Press, 2003.

Cimprich, John. "Slave Behavior during the Federal Occupation of Tennessee, 1862–1865." *Historian* 44 (1982): 335–46.

Clarke, Erskine. *Wrestlin' Jacob: A Portrait of Religion in the Old South.* Atlanta: John Knox Press, 1979.

Clayton, Ronnie W. *Mother Wit: The Ex-slave Narratives of the Louisiana Writers' Project.* New York: Peter Lang, 1990.

Clebsch, William A., ed. *Journals of the Protestant Episcopal Church in the Confederate States of America.* Austin, TX: Church Historical Society, 1962.

Clendinnen, Inga. *Ambivalent Conquests: Maya and Spaniard in Yucatan, 1517–1570.* Cambridge: Cambridge University Press, 1987.

Coleman, Will. *Tribal Talk: Black Theology, Hermeneutics, and African/American Ways of "Telling the Story."* University Park: Pennsylvania State University Press, 2000.

Cornelius, Janet Duitsman. *Slave Missions and the Black Church in the Antebellum South.* Columbia: University of South Carolina Press, 1999.

Crabtree, Beth G., and James W. Patton, eds. *"Journal of a Secesh Lady": The Diary of Catherine Ann Devereux Edmondston, 1860–1866.* Raleigh, NC: Division of Archives and History, 1979.

Cravath, E. M. "The Necessity of Endowing Our Larger Institutions." *American Missionary* 40, no. 11 (November 1886): 316–19.

Creel, Margaret Washington. *A Peculiar People: Slave Religion and Community Culture among the Gullahs.* New York: New York University Press, 1988.

Davis, Rod. *American Voudou: Journey into a Hidden World.* Denton: University of North Texas Press, 1998.

DeBoer, Clara Merritt. *His Truth Is Marching On: African Americans Who Taught the Freedmen for the American Missionary Association, 1861–1877.* New York: Garland, 1995.

Deetz, James. *Flowerdew Hundred: The Archaeology of a Virginia Plantation, 1619–1864.* Charlottesville: University Press of Virginia, 1993.

Dennard, David C. "Religion in the Quarters: A Study of Slave Preachers in the Antebellum South, 1800–1860." Dissertation, Northwestern University–Illinois, 1983.

Deren, Maya. *Divine Horsemen: The Living Gods of Haiti.* London: Thames & Hudson, 1953.

Diouf, Sylviane A. *Servants of Allah: African Muslims Enslaved in the Americas.* New York: New York University Press, 1998.

Douglass, Frederick. *Narrative of the Life of Frederick Douglas, an American Slave.* Ed. Houston Baker. 1845. Reprint, Middlesex, Eng.: Penguin Classics, 1986.

————. *Life and Times of Frederick Douglass.* 1892. Reprint, London: Collier-Macmillan, 1962.

Drago, Edmund L. "How Sherman's March through Georgia Affected the Slaves." *Georgia Historical Quarterly* 57 (1973): 361–75.

Drew, Benjamin. *A North-Side View of Slavery.* Boston: John P. Jewett & Company, 1856.

Du Bois, W. E. B. *The Souls of Black Folk.* 1903. Reprint, Greenwich, CT: Fawcett, 1964.

Earl, Riggins R., Jr. *Dark Symbols, Obscure Signs: God, Self, and Community in the Slave Mind.* Maryknoll, NY: Orbis, 1993.

Elizabeth. *Elizabeth, a Colored Minister of the Gospel Born in Slavery.* Philadelphia: Tract Association of Friends, 1889.

Elkins, Stanley. *Slavery: A Problem in American Institutional and Intellectual Life.* 3rd ed. Chicago: University of Chicago Press, 1976.

Epstein, Dena J. "Slave Music in the United States before 1860: A Survey of Sources, Pts. 1–2." *Music Library Association Notes* 20 (Spring–Summer 1963): 195–212, 377–90.

Federal Writers' Project. *Born in Slavery: Slave Narratives from the Federal Writers' Project, 1936–38.* American Memory Collection. http://memory.loc.gov/ammem/snhtml/snhome.html.

Ferebee, L. R. *A Brief History of the Slave Life of Rev. L. R. Ferebee, and the Battles of Life, and Four Years of His Ministerial Life.* Raleigh, NC: Edwards, Broughton & Company, 1882.

Ferguson, Leland. *Uncommon Ground: Archaeology and Early African America.* Washington, DC: Smithsonian, 1992.

Ferris, William. "Voodoo." In *Encyclopedia of Southern Culture,* ed. Charles Wilson and William Ferris, 492–93. Chapel Hill: University of North Carolina Press, 1989.

Flynt, Wayne. *Alabama Baptists: Southern Baptists in the Heart of Dixie.* Tuscaloosa: University of Alabama Press, 1998.

Forten, Charlotte. "Life on the Sea Islands." In *Two Black Teachers during the Civil War,* by Lewis C. Lockwood. New York: Arno Press, 1969. First published in *Atlantic Monthly,* May–June 1864.

Foster, Henry B. *History of the Tuscaloosa County Baptist Association, 1834–1934.* Tuscaloosa: Weatherford Printing, 1934.

Fountain, Daniel, "Historians and Historical Archaeology: Slave Sites." *Journal of Interdisciplinary History* 26 (Summer 1995): 66–77.

Frazier, Thomas. "Religion and Women." In *Encyclopedia of Southern Culture,* ed. Charles Wilson and William Ferris, 1563. Chapel Hill: University of North Carolina Press, 1989.

Friedman, Jean E. *The Enclosed Garden: Women and Community in the Evangeli-*

cal South, 1830–1900. Chapel Hill: University of North Carolina Press, 1985.

Frey, Sylvia R., and Betty Wood. *Come Shouting to Zion: African American Protestantism in the American South and British Caribbean to 1830.* Chapel Hill: University of North Carolina Press, 1998.

Fulop, Timothy E., and Albert J. Raboteau, eds. *African-American Religion: Interpretive Essays in History and Culture.* New York: Routledge, 1997.

Furman, Jan, ed. *Slavery in the Clover Bottoms: John McCline's Narrative of His Life during Slavery and the Civil War.* Knoxville: University of Tennessee Press, 1998.

Gannett, W. C. "The Freedmen at Port Royal." *North American Review* 101 (July 1865): 1–28.

Garbarino, James, et al. *Children and Families in the Social Environment.* 2nd ed. New York: Aldine De Gruyter, 1992.

Gates, Henry Louis, ed. *The Classic Slave Narratives.* New York: New American Library, 1987.

Gaustad, Edwin S., ed. *A Documentary History of Religion in America to the Civil War.* Grand Rapids, MI: Eerdman's, 1982.

Genovese, Eugene D. *Roll, Jordan, Roll: The World the Slaves Made.* New York: Vintage, 1974.

———. *A Consuming Fire: The Fall of the Confederacy in the Mind of the White Christian South.* Athens: University of Georgia Press, 1998.

Gomez, Michael A. "Muslims in Early America." *Journal of Southern History* 40 (November 1994): 671–710.

———. *Exchanging Our Country Marks: The Transformation of African Identities in the Colonial and Antebellum South.* Chapel Hill: University Press of North Carolina, 1998.

Gorn, Elliot J. "Black Spirits: The Ghostlore of Afro-American Slaves." *American Quarterly* 36 (Fall 1984): 549–65.

Grandy, Moses. *Narrative of the Life of Moses Grandy, Late a Slave in the United States of America.* Boston: Oliver Johnson, 1844.

Greene, Glen Lee. *House upon a Rock: About Southern Baptists in Louisiana.* Alexandria, LA: Executive Board of the Louisiana Baptist Convention, 1973.

Greven, Philip. *The Protestant Temperament: Patterns of Child-Rearing, Religious Experience, and the Self in Early America.* New York: Knopf, 1977.

Grimes, William. *The Life of William Grimes, the Runaway Slave, Written by Himself.* New York: N.p., 1825.

Handler, Jerome S., Frederick Lange, and Charles Orser Jr. "Carnelian Beads in Necklaces from a Slave Cemetery in Barbados, West Indies," *Ornament* 3 (1979): 15–18.

Handy, M. P. "Witchcraft among the Negroes," *Appleton's Journal* 8, no. 194 (December 1872): 666–67.

Harris, William C., ed. *"In the Country of the Enemy": The Civil War Reports of a Massachusetts Corporal.* Gainesville: University Press of Florida, 1999.

Harrison, W. P., ed. *The Gospel among the Slaves.* Nashville: Publishing House of the M. E. Church, South, 1893.

Harvey, Paul. *Freedom's Coming: Religious Culture and the Shaping of the South from the Civil War through the Civil Rights Era.* Chapel Hill: University of North Carolina Press, 2005.

———. "'These Untutored Masses': The Campaign for Respectability among White and Black Evangelicals in the American South, 1870–1930." In *Southern Crossroads: Perspectives on Religion and Culture,* eds. Walter Conser Jr. and Rodger Payne. Lexington: University Press of Kentucky, 2008.

Hefner, Robert, ed. *Conversion to Christianity: Historical and Anthropological Perspectives on a Great Transformation.* Berkeley: University of California Press, 1993.

Herskovits, Melville J. *The Myth of the Negro Past.* With a new preface by the author. 1958. Third printing, Boston: Beacon Press, 1964.

Heyrman, Christine Leigh. *Southern Cross: The Beginnings of the Bible Belt.* Chapel Hill: University of North Carolina Press, 1997.

Hicks, William. *History of Louisiana Negro Baptists and Early American Beginnings from 1804–1914.* Lafayette: Center for Louisiana Studies, 1998.

Higginbotham, Evelyn Brooks. *Righteous Discontent: The Women's Movement in the Black Baptist Church, 1880–1920.* Cambridge, MA: Harvard University Press, 1993.

Higginson, Thomas Wentworth. *Army Life in a Black Regiment.* Boston: Fields, Asgood, & Company, 1870.

Hildebrand, Reginald F. *The Times Were Strange and Stirring: Methodist Preachers and the Crisis of Emancipation.* Durham, NC: Duke University Press, 1995.

Holloway, Joseph E., ed. *Africanisms in American Culture.* Bloomington: Indiana University Press, 1991.

Horton, Robin. *Patterns of Thought in Africa and the West: Essays on Magic, Religion, and Science.* Cambridge: Cambridge University Press, 1997.

Houk, James. "Anthropological Theory and the Breakdown of Eclectic Folk Religions." *Journal for the Scientific Study of Religion* 35, no. 4 (1996): 442–47.

Hughes, Louis. *Thirty Years a Slave. From Bondage to Freedom. The Institution of Slavery as Seen on the Plantation and in the Home of the Planter.* Milwaukee: South Side Printing, 1897.

Hume, Ivor Noel. "An Indian Ware of the Colonial Period." *Quarterly Bulletin of the Archaeological Society of Virginia* 17 (1962): 2–14.

Hurston, Zora Neale. *Mules and Men.* 1935. Reprint, New York: Harper Perennial, 1990.

Hyatt, Harry Middleton. *Hoodoo-Conjuration-Witchcraft-Rootwork: Beliefs Ac-*

cepted by Many Negroes and White Persons, These Being Orally Recorded among Blacks and Whites. Hannibal, MO: Western, 1970.

Ikenga-Metuh, Emefie. "The Shattered Microcosm: A Critical Survey of Explanations of Conversion in Africa." In Petersen, *Religion, Development, and African Identity*, 11–27. Uppsala: Scandinavian Institute of African Studies, 1987.

Jackson, John Andrew. *The Experience of a Slave in South Carolina.* London: Passmore & Alabaster, 1862.

Jamison, Monroe F. *Autobiography and Work of Bishop M. F. Jamison, D.D. ("Uncle Joe"), Editor, Publisher, and Church Extension Secretary; a Narration of His Whole Career from the Cradle to the Bishopric of the Colored M. E. Church in America.* Nashville: Publishing House of the M.E. Church, 1912.

Johnson, Alonzo, and Paul Jersild. *"Ain't Gonna Lay My 'Ligion Down": African American Religion in the South.* Columbia: University of South Carolina Press, 1996.

Johnson, Guy. *Drums and Shadows: Survival Studies among the Georgia Coastal Negroes.* Athens: University of Georgia Press, 1940.

Johnson, Paul E., ed. *African-American Christianity: Essays in History.* Berkeley: University of California Press, 1994.

Johnson, Thomas L. *Twenty-Eight Years a Slave in Virginia, afterwards, at Forty Years of Age, a Student in Spurgeon's College, Missionary in Africa, Evangelist in England.* Bournemouth: W. Mate & Sons, 1909.

Johnson, William Courtland. "A Delusive Clothing": Christian Conversion in the Antebellum Slave Community." *Journal of Negro History* 82 (Summer 1997): 295–311.

Jones, Charles Colcock. *The Religious Instruction of the Negroes in the United States.* Savannah, GA: Published by Thomas Purse, 1842.

———. *Catechism of Scripture, Doctrine, and Practice, for Families and Sabbath Schools, Designed also for the Oral Instruction of Colored Persons.* Savannah, GA: T. Purse & Co., 1844.

———. "Suggestions on the Religious Instruction of the Negroes in the Southern States." *Princeton Review* 20 (January 1848): 1–30.

———. *Religious Instruction of the Negroes: An Address Delivered before the General Assembly of the Presbyterian Church, at Augusta, Ga, December 10, 1861.* Richmond, VA: Presbyterian Committee of Publication, 1862.

Jones, Friday. *Days of Bondage: Autobiography of Friday Jones. Being a Brief Narrative of His Trials and Tribulations in Slavery.* Washington, DC: Commercial Pub. Co., 1883.

Jones, George Noble, Ulrich B. Phillips, and James David Glunt. *Florida Plantation Records from the Papers of George Noble Jones.* St. Louis: Missouri Historical Society, 1927.

Jones, J. William. *Christ in the Camp; or, Religion in Lee's Army.* Richmond, VA: B. F. Johnson, 1888.

Jones, Thomas H. *The Experience of Thomas H. Jones, Who Was a Slave for Forty-Three Years.* Boston: Bazin & Chandler, 1862.

Jordan, Winthrop D. *Tumult and Silence at Second Creek: An Inquiry into a Civil War Slave Conspiracy.* Rev. ed. Baton Rouge: Louisiana State University Press, 1995.

Joyner, Charles. *Down by the Riverside: A South Carolina Slave Community.* Urbana: University of Illinois Press, 1984.

———. "History as Ritual: Rites of Power and Resistance on the Slave Plantation." *Australasian Journal of American Studies* 5 (1986): 3.

Kemble, Frances Anne. *Journal of a Residence on a Georgian Plantation in 1838–39.* Ed. John Scott. 1863. New York: Knopf, 1961.

King, Wilma. *Stolen Childhood: Slave Youth in Nineteenth-Century America.* Bloomington: Indiana University Press, 1995.

Kolchin, Peter. *American Slavery, 1619–1877.* New York: Hill & Wang, 1993.

Leone, Mark P., and Gladys-Marie Fry. "Conjuring in the Big House Kitchen: An Interpretation of African-American Belief Systems Based on the Uses of Archaeology and Folklore Sources." *Journal of American Folklore* 112, no. 445 (Summer 1999): 372–403.

Levine, Lawrence. *Black Culture and Black Consciousness: Afro-American Folk Thought from Slavery to Freedom.* Oxford: Oxford University Press, 1977.

Loguen, Jermain Wesley. *The Rev. J. W. Loguen, As a Slave and as a Freedman.* Syracuse: J. G. K. Truair & Company, 1859.

Loveland, Anne C. *Southern Evangelicals and the Social Order, 1800–1860.* Baton Rouge: Louisiana State University Press, 1980.

Marrs, Elijah P. *Life and History of the Rev. Elijah P. Marrs, First Pastor of Beargrass Baptist Church, and Author.* Louisville: Bradley & Gilbert Co., 1885.

Marsden, George. *Fundamentalism and American Culture: The Shaping of Twentieth-Century Evangelicalism, 1870–1925.* Oxford: Oxford University Press, 1980.

Martin, B. G. "Sapelo Island's Arabic Document: The 'Bilali Diary' in Context." *Georgia Historical Quarterly* 77 (Fall 1994): 589–601.

Martin, Sandy Dwayne. *For God and Race: The Religious and Political Leadership of AMEZ Bishop James Walker Hood.* Columbia: University of South Carolina Press, 1999.

Mason, Isaac. *Life of Isaac Mason as a Slave.* Worcester, MA: N.p., 1893.

Mathews, Donald G. *Religion in the Old South.* Chicago: University of Chicago Press, 1977.

Mbiti, John S. *African Religions and Philosophy.* Garden City, NY: Anchor, 1970.

———. *Introduction to African Religion.* 2nd ed. Oxford: Heinemann, 1991.

McCray, S. J. *Life of Mary F. McCray Born and Raised a Slave in the State of Kentucky. By Her Husband and Son.* Lima, OH: N.p., 1898.

McDaniel, George. "Housing." In *Dictionary of Afro-American Slavery*, eds. Randall Miller and John David Smith, 343. New York: Greenwood, 1988.

McKee, Larry. "The Earth Is Their Witness." *The Sciences* 35 (March/April 1995): 36–41.

McWhiney, Grady, Warner O. Moore Jr., and Robert F. Pace, eds. *"Fear God and Walk Humbly": The Agricultural Journal of James Mallory, 1843–1877.* Tuscaloosa: University of Alabama Press, 1997.

Metraux, Alfred. *Voodoo in Haiti.* With an introduction by Sidney Mintz. 1959. New York: Schocken, 1972.

Middleton, John Allen. *Directory and Pre-1900 Historical Survey of South Carolina's Black Baptists.* Columbia, SC: J. A. Middleton, 1992.

Miller, Randall M. *"Dear Master": Letters of a Slave Family.* Ithaca, NY: Cornell University Press, 1978.

Miller, Randall, Harry Stout, and Charles Wilson, eds. *Religion and the American Civil War.* New York: Oxford University Press, 1998.

Miller, Reverend C. W. "Baptism and Church Membership of Children." *Quarterly Review of the Methodist Episcopal Church, South* 15 (April 1861): 256–69.

Mintz, Sidney, and Richard Price. *The Birth of African-American Culture: An Anthropological Perspective.* Boston: Beacon, 1992.

Montgomery, William E. *Under Their Own Vine and Fig Tree: The African-American Church in the South, 1865–1900.* Baton Rouge: Louisiana State University Press, 1993.

Morgan, Edmund S. *The Puritan Family: Religion and Domestic Relations in Seventeenth-Century New England.* New York: Harper & Row, 1966.

Morgan, Philip D. *Slave Counterpoint: Black Culture in the Eighteenth-Century Chesapeake and Lowcountry.* Chapel Hill: University of North Carolina Press, 1998.

Murphy, Joseph M. *Working the Spirit: Ceremonies of the African Diaspora.* Boston: Beacon, 1994.

Murphy, Larry G. "Religion in the African-American Community." In *Encyclopedia of African-American Religions*, ed. Larry G. Murphy, J. Gordon Melton, and Gary L. Ward, xxxi–xxxv. New York: Garland, 1993.

Myers, Robert M., ed. *The Children of Pride: Selected Letters of the Family of the Rev. Dr. Charles Colcock Jones from the Years 1860–1868.* New Haven, CT: Yale University Press, 1984.

Myrdal, Gunnar. *An American Dilemma: The Negro Problem and Modern Democracy.* New York: Harper & Row, 1944.

New England Educational Commission for Freedmen. *Extracts from Letters of*

Teachers and Superintendents of the New England Educational Commission for Freedmen. 4th series. Boston: David Clapp, 1864.

Nichols, Thomas L. *Forty Years of American Life.* Vol. 2. London: John Maxwell & Company, 1864.

Oates, Stephen B. *The Fires of Jubilee: Nat Turner's Fierce Rebellion.* New York: New American Library, 1975.

Olmsted, Frederick Law. *A Journey in the Seaboard Slave States; with Remarks on Their Economy.* London: Sampson, Low, Son & Co., 1856.

————. *The Cotton Kingdom: A Traveller's Observations on Cotton and Slavery in the American Slave States, 1853–1861.* Ed. Arthur M. Schlesinger. New York: Da Capo, 1996.

Orser, Charles E. "The Archaeology of African-American Slave Religion in the Antebellum South." *Cambridge Archaeological Journal* 4, no. 1 (1994): 33–45.

————. "The Archaeology of African American Slave Religion in the Antebellum South." In *Southern Crossroads: Perspectives on Religion and Culture,* eds. Walter Conser Jr. and Rodger Payne. Lexington: University Press of Kentucky, 2008.

Owen, Christopher H. *The Sacred Flame of Love: Methodism and Society in Nineteenth-Century Georgia.* Athens: University of Georgia Press, 1998.

Ownby, Ted. *Subduing Satan: Religion, Recreation, and Manhood in the Rural South, 1865–1920.* Chapel Hill: University of North Carolina Press, 1990.

Parker, Allen. *Recollections of Slavery Times.* Worcester, MA: Chas. W. Burbank & Co., 1895.

Parrinder, Geoffrey. *African Traditional Religion.* Westport, CT: Greenwood, 1976.

Parsons, Talcott, and Robert F. Bales. *Family Socialization and Interaction Process.* Glencoe, IL: Free Press, 1955.

Patten, M. Drake. "Mankala and Minkisi: Possible Evidence of African American Folk Beliefs and Practices." *African American Archaeology* 6 (1992): 5–7.

Paxton, Rev. W. E. *A History of the Baptists of Louisiana from the Earliest Times to the Present.* St. Louis: C. R. Barns, 1888.

Pearson, Elizabeth Ware, ed. *Letters from Port Royal, 1862–1868.* 1906. Reprint, New York: Arno Press, 1969.

Pennington, James W. C. *The Fugitive Blacksmith.* 2nd ed. London: Charles Gilpin, 1849.

Perdue, Charles L., Jr., et al., eds. *Weevils in the Wheat: Interviews with Virginia Ex-Slaves.* Charlottesville: University of Virginia Press, 1976.

Petersen, K. Holst, ed. *Religion, Development, and African Identity.* Uppsala: Scandinavian Institute of African Studies, 1987.

Phillips, U. B. *American Negro Slavery: A Survey of the Supply, Employment and*

Control of Negro Labor as Determined by the Plantation Regime. 1918. Reprint, Baton Rouge: Louisiana State University Press, 1966.

Pinn, Anthony. *Varieties of African American Religious Experience.* Minneapolis: Fortress Press, 1998.

Pogue, Dennis, and Esther White. "Summary Report on the 'House for Families' Slave Quarter Site (44FX762/40–47), Mount Vernon Plantation, Mount Vernon, Virginia." *Quarterly Bulletin of the Archaeological Society of Virginia* 44 (1991): 189–206.

Polehmus, Richard R. "Archaeological Investigation of the Tellico Blockhouse Site (40MR50): A Federal Military and Trade Complex." Unpublished report submitted to the Tennessee Valley Authority, 1977.

Pollock, Linda A. *Forgotten Children: Parent-Child Relations from 1500 to 1900.* Cambridge: Cambridge University Press, 1983.

Puckett, Newbell Niles. *Folk Beliefs of the Southern Negro.* Chapel Hill: University of North Carolina Press, 1926.

Raboteau, Albert. *Slave Religion: The "Invisible Institution" in the Antebellum South.* New York: Oxford University Press, 1978.

Randolph, Peter. *Sketches of Slave Life; or, Illustrations of the "Peculiar Institution."* Boston: Peter Randolph, 1855.

———. *Slave Cabin to the Pulpit.* Boston: N.p., 1893.

Rawick, George, ed. *The American Slave: A Composite Autobiography.* Vols. 2–19; Supplement Series 1, vols. 1–12; Supplement Series 2, vols. 1–10. Westport, CT: Greenwood, 1973–1981.

Redkey, Edwin S. "Black Chaplains in the Union Army." *Civil War History* 33 (1987): 331–50.

Reilly, Wayne E., ed. *Sarah Jane Foster, Teacher of the Freedmen: A Diary and Letters.* Charlottesville: University Press of Virginia, 1990.

Reis, Joao Jose. *Slave Rebellion in Brazil: The Muslim Uprising of 1835 in Bahia.* Translated by Arthur Brakel. Baltimore: Johns Hopkins University Press, 1993.

Robinson, Jean W. "Black Healers during the Colonial Period and Early Nineteenth Century America." Ph.D. dissertation, Southern Illinois University, 1979.

Robinson, W. H. *From Log Cabin to the Pulpit, or Fifteen Years in Slavery.* Eau Claire, WI: James H. Tift, 1913.

Roper, Moses. *A Narrative of the Adventures and Escape of Moses Roper, from American Slavery.* Philadelphia: Merrihew & Gunn, Printers, 1838.

Ross, Fred A. *Slavery Ordained of God.* 1857. Reprint, Miami: Mnemosyne, 1969.

Russell, Aaron E. "Material Culture and African-American Spirituality at the Hermitage." *Historical Archaeology* 31, no. 2 (1997): 63–80.

S. M. P. "Voodooism in Tennessee." *Atlantic Monthly* 64, no. 383 (September 1889): 376–80.

St. Amant, C. Penrose. *A Short History of Louisiana Baptists.* Nashville: Broadman, 1948.

Samford, Patricia. "Searching for West African Cultural Meanings in the Archaeological Record." *African-American Archaeology* 12 (Winter 1994): 2–7.

Sawyer, George. *Southern Institutions; or, An Inquiry into the Origin and Early Prevalence of Slavery and the Slave-Trade: With an Analysis of the Laws, History, and Government of the Institution in the Principal Nations, Ancient and Modern, from the Earliest Ages Down to the Present Time with Notes and Comments in Defence of the Southern Institutions.* Philadelphia: J. B. Lippincott, 1858.

Saxon, Lyle, Edward Dreyer, and Robert Tallant, eds. *Gumbo Ya-Ya: A Collection of Louisiana Folk Tales.* Boston: Houghton Mifflin, 1945.

Schwartz, Marie J. *Born in Bondage: Growing Up Enslaved in the Antebellum South.* Cambridge, MA: Harvard University Press, 2001.

Seabury, Caroline. *The Diary of Caroline Seabury, 1854–1863.* Ed. Suzanne L. Bunkers. Madison: University of Wisconsin Press, 1991.

Sehat, David. "The Civilizing Mission of Booker T. Washington." *Journal of Southern History* 73, no. 2 (May 2007): 323–62.

Sernett, Milton C. *Black Religion and American Evangelicalism: White Protestants, Plantation Missions and the Flowering of Negro Christianity, 1787–1865.* ATLA Monograph Series, no. 7. Metuchen, NJ: Scarecrow Press, 1975.

Shattuck, Gardiner H., Jr. *A Shield and Hiding Place: The Religious Life of the Civil War Armies.* Macon, GA: Mercer University Press, 1987.

Singleton, Theresa. "The Archaeology of Slavery in North America." *Annual Review of Anthropology* 24 (1995): 119–40.

Smith, Charles Spencer. *A History of the African Methodist Episcopal Church: Being a Volume Supplemental to A History of the African Methodist Episcopal Church, by Daniel Alexander Payne, D.D., LL.D., Late one of Its Bishops: Chronicling the Principal Events in the Advance of the African Methodist Episcopal Church from 1856 to 1922.* Philadelphia: Book Concern of the A.M.E. Church, 1922.

Smith, James L. *Autobiography of James L. Smith, Including, Also, Reminiscences of Slave Life, Recollections of the War, Education of Freedmen, Causes of the Exodus, etc.* Norwich: Press of the Bulleting Co., 1881.

Smith, John David. *Black Judas: William Hannibal Thomas and "The American Negro."* Athens: University of Georgia Press, 2000.

Smith, Timothy. "Religion and Ethnicity in America." *American Historical Review* 83 (December 1978): 1155–85.

Sobel, Mechal. *Trabelin' On: The Slave Journey to an Afro-Baptist Faith*. Princeton, NJ: Princeton University Press, 1979.

Steward, Austin. *Twenty-Two Years a Slave and Forty Years a Freeman*. Rochester, NY: William Alling, 1857.

Stine, Linda, Melanie Cabak, and Mark D. Groover. "Blue Beads as African-American Cultural Symbols." *Historical Archaeology* 30, no. 3 (1996): 49–75.

Stowe, Harriet Beecher. "Our Florida Plantation." *Atlantic Monthly* 43, no. 259 (May 1879): 641–50.

Stowell, Daniel W. *Rebuilding Zion: The Religious Reconstruction of the South, 1863–1877*. New York: Oxford University Press, 1998.

Stroyer, Jacob. *My Life in the South*. Salem, MA: Newcomb & Gauss, 1898.

Stuckey, Sterling. *Slave Culture: Nationalist Theory and the Foundations of Black America*. New York: Oxford University Press, 1987.

"Studies in the South." *Atlantic Monthly* 50, no. 300 (October 1882): 479.

Swint, Henry L., ed. *Dear Ones at Home: Letters from Contraband Camps*. Nashville: Vanderbilt University Press, 1966.

Taylor, Joe Gray. *Louisiana Reconstructed, 1863–1877*. Baton Rouge: Louisiana State University Press, 1974.

Teacher in the South. "What Shall We Believe about the Negro?" *American Missionary* 45, no. 9 (September 1891): 316–18.

Thanet, Octave. "Plantation Life in Arkansas." *Atlantic Monthly* 68, no. 405 (July 1891), 32–49.

Thomas, James. *From Tennessee Slave to St. Louis Entrepreneur: The Autobiography of James Thomas*. Ed. Loren Schweninger. Columbia: University of Missouri Press, 1984.

Thomas, William Hannibal. *The American Negro: What He Was, What He Is, and What He May Become. Critical and Practical Discussion*. London: Macmillan, 1901.

Thompson, John. *The Life of John Thompson, a Fugitive Slave; Containing His History of 25 Years in Bondage, and His Providential Escape*. Worchester, MA: John Thompson, 1856.

Thompson, Robert. *Flash of the Spirit: African and Afro-American Art and Philosophy*. New York: Random House, 1983.

Travis, Joseph. *Rev. Joseph Travis, A.M., A Member of the Memphis Annual Conference. Embracing a Succinct History of the Methodist Episcopal Church, South; Particularly in Part of Western Virginia, the Carolinas, Georgia, Alabama, and Mississippi. With Several Short of Several Local Preachers, and an Address to His Friends*. Nashville: E. Stevenson & F.A. Owen, Agents of the Methodist Episcopal Church, South, 1856.

Tylor, E. B. "On the Survival of Savage Thought in Modern Civilization, Part I." *Appleton's Journal* 1, no. 18 (July 1869): 566–68.

Vlach, John. *The Afro-American Tradition in Decorative Arts*. Cleveland: Cleveland Museum of Art, 1978.

Voeks, Robert. "African Medicine and Magic in the Americas." *Geographical Review* 83, no. 1 (1993): 66–78.

Walker, Cam. "Corinth: The Story of a Contraband Camp." *Civil War History* 20 (1974): 5–22.

Walker, Clarence E. *A Rock in a Weary Land: The African Methodist Episcopal Church during the Civil War and Reconstruction*. Baton Rouge: Louisiana State University Press, 1982.

Warner, Charles Dudley. *Studies in the South and West and Comments on Canada*. New York: Harper & Brothers, 1889.

Washington, Booker T. "The Colored Ministry: Its Defects and Needs." *Christian Union* 42 (August 14, 1890): 199–200.

———. "The Awakening of the Negro." *Atlantic Monthly* 78, no. 467 (September 1896): 322–32.

Washington, Booker T., and W. E. B. Du Bois. *The Negro in the South: His Economic Progress in Relation to His Moral and Religious Development*. Philadelphia: G. W. Jacobs, 1907.

Washington, James Melvin. *Frustrated Fellowship: The Black Baptist Quest for Social Power*. Macon, GA: Mercer University Press, 1986.

Waters, Donald, ed. *Strange Ways and Sweet Dreams: Afro-American Folklore from the Hampton Institute*. Boston: G. K. Hall, 1983.

Watts, Isaac. *Dr. Watt's Plain and Easy Catechism for Children to Which Are Added Forms of Prayer, Adapted to the Smallest Capacities*. Cambridge, MA: William Hilliard, 1806.

Weiner, Marli F. *Mistresses and Slaves: Plantation Women in South Carolina, 1830–1880*. Urbana: University of Illinois Press, 1998.

Wheeler, Edward L. "Beyond One Man: A General Survey of Black Baptist Church History." *Review and Expositor* 70 (Summer 1973): 309–19.

White, Heather Rachelle. "'The Glory of Southern Christianity': Methodism and the Mission to the Slaves." *Methodist History* 39, no. 2 (January 2001): 108–21.

Wightman, William M. *Life of William Capers, D.D., One of the Bishops of the Methodist Episcopal Church South; Including an Autobiography*. Nashville: Southern Methodist Publishing House, 1859.

Wilkie, Laurie A. "Magic and Empowerment on the Plantation: An Archaeological Consideration of African-American Worldview." *Southeastern Archaeology* 14 (Winter 1995): 136–48.

Williams, Isaac. *Aunt Sally; or, The Cross the Way of Freedom. A Narrative of the Slave-life and Purchase of the Mother of Rev. Isaac Williams of Detroit, Michigan*. Cincinnati: American Reform Tract and Book Society, 1858.

————. *Sunshine and Shadow of Slave Life*. East Saginaw, MI: Evening News Printing and Binding House, 1885.

Williams, James. *Narrative of James Williams, an American Slave; Who Was for Several Years a Driver on a Cotton Plantation in Alabama*. New York: American Anti-Slavery Society, 1838.

Willis, John C. "From the Dictates of Pride to the Paths of Righteousness: Slave Honor and Christianity in Antebellum Virginia." In *The Edge of the South*, eds. Edward Ayers and John C. Willis, 37–55. Charlottesville: University Press of Virginia, 1991.

Yakubik, Jill-Karen, et al. "Archaeological Data Recovery at Ashland-Belle Helene Plantation (16AN26), Ascension Parish, Louisiana." Unpublished report on file with Louisiana Department of Culture, Recreation, and Tourism, Division of Archaeology, 1994.

Yinger, J. Milton. *Religion, Society, and the Individual: An Introduction to the Sociology of Religion*. New York: Macmillan, 1957.

Young, Amy L. "Archaeological Evidence of African-Style Ritual and Healing Practices in the Upland South." *Tennessee Anthropologist* 21 (Fall 1996): 139–55.

Zahan, Dominique. *The Religion, Spirituality, and Thought of Traditional Africa*. Chicago: University of Chicago Press, 1979.

Zanca, Kenneth J., ed. *American Catholics and Slavery, 1789–1866: An Anthology of Primary Documents*. Lanham, MD: University Press of America, 1994.

Zipf, Karin L. "'Among These American Heathens': Congregationalist Missionaries and African American Evangelicals during Reconstruction, 1865–1878." *North Carolina Historical Review* 74 (April 1997): 111–34.

INDEX